BORE NO MORE! 2

with a foreword by
Mike Nappa

Vital
MINISTRY
Loveland, Colorado

Bore No More! 2

CREDITS
Contributing Authors: Amy Simpson, Trevor Simpson, Dennis R. McLaughlin, Paul Woods, Lori Haynes Niles, Ken Niles, Mikal Keefer, Michael Warden, Pete Briscoe, Dary Northrop, and Jere McCully
Acquisitions Editor: Dave Thornton
Editor: Dennis R. McLaughlin
Creative Development Editor: Paul Woods
Chief Creative Officer: Joani Schultz
Copy Editor: Candace McMahan
Art Director: Kari K. Monson
Designers: Helen H. Lannis and Kari K. Monson
Cover Designer: Liz Howe
Computer Graphic Artist: Joyce Douglas
Illustrators: Shelley Dieterichs-Morrison and Leslie Dunlap
Cartoonists: John McPherson and Rob Portlock
Production Manager: Peggy Naylor

Library of Congress Cataloging-in-Publication Data
Bore no more! 2 / with a foreword by Mike Nappa.
      p.   cm.
    Continues: Bore no more! / by Mike & Amy Nappa.
    Includes index.
    ISBN 0-7644-2109-3 (alk. paper)
    1. Homiletical illustrations. I. Nappa, Mike, 1963- Bore no
more!
BV4225.2.B67   1998
252' .08--dc21   98-38278
                                          CIP

10 9 8 7 6 5 4 3 2 1   08 07 06 05 04 03 02 01 00 99

Printed in the United States of America.

Contents

Foreword

Anything can happen during a church service. Anything!

It was in a synagogue that Jesus argued with the Pharisees about healing a man with a shriveled hand (Matthew 12:9-14). It was during an assembly of first-century believers that the Holy Spirit swept mightily into the hearts and lives of God's people (Acts 2). And it was during a church service that the Apostle Paul bored someone to death (literally!), then raised him from the dead and kept on preaching (Acts 20:9-12).

As I said, anything can happen during a church service. Unfortunately, monotony, listlessness, and forgetfulness are all too often among those occurrences. At least that was my experience a few years ago. The church my wife, Amy, and I were attending had just welcomed a new pastor. He was (and is!) a genuinely nice man; a solid Christian; and a leader with a heart for God and a desire to see people grow stronger in their faith. The trouble began when I noticed that I was unable to maintain my concentration whenever he stood to preach.

I've given my share of sermons and have served on the ministry staff of a few churches as well. I know that the listener does share in the responsibility for getting something out of a sermon. So to help maintain my focus, I started brainstorming during each Sunday sermon. I asked myself, "What could my pastor do today to illustrate this point in a creative way? What could he do to capture the attention of everyone in this room?" I began listening for his sermon hooks and jotting down ideas that he could have used to illustrate his points. I tried to think of ideas that would be attention-grabbing, age-appropriate, interesting, and involving. It was actually kind of fun!

Pretty soon Amy wondered what I was scribbling in the weekly bulletins. When I showed her my ideas, she said, "You know, if you had enough of these, you could make a book of interactive sermon illustrations for pastors and speakers." The seed was planted. Amy and I started working together on ideas and testing them at speaking engagements, women's groups, Bible studies, church meetings, and everywhere else we could.

As a result, Amy and I wrote a book called *Bore No More!* By God's grace and through your support, *Bore No More!* sold out six weeks after its release in 1995. Unfortunately, our schedules didn't allow us time to write a sequel. We did, however, encourage Group Publishing, Inc. to develop a second volume.

To our delight, we recently read through the finished manuscript of *Bore No More! 2*. We were impressed with the caliber of authors Group had chosen to write the book. These folks not only excel at creative communication, but most are battle-tested veterans who know what it's like to work on the front lines of ministry. We were quite thrilled at the exciting possibilities these authors have dreamed up for you to use. (If the truth is to be known, they probably did a better job writing this book than we would have!)

Now the rest is up to you. You have only a few precious moments each week to influence your listeners with the truths of Scripture. So our prayer is that God will work through you to maximize the impact of his Word through an unforgettable, audience-involving idea from this book. It's as easy as turning the page. And remember, anything can happen during a church service...

—MIKE NAPPA

Introduction

It's sad but true that while "parishioners often cite the sermon as the pinnacle of the worship service...they retain very little from it" (Thom and Joani Schultz, *Why Nobody Learns Much of Anything at Church: And How to Fix It*).

Does this suggest that preaching is a dying art? or that the sermon is on its way out? Hardly!

Yet, why aren't preachers getting the results they desire from their sermons? Why are listeners complaining that they are bored? Why are congregation members saying they're ready for their pastors to try something new?

The answer, at least in part, is revealed in a recent book by Robert N. Nash. In *An 8-Track Church in a CD World,* Nash reminds us that "we have moved from record albums and 8-track tapes to compact discs, from electric typewriters to Pentium computers, and from board games to SuperNintendo."

It's not that the people in our churches have gone astray. It's just that the way their minds process information has evolved over time. The truth is, many young Christians have never heard of an 8-track tape. Yet, many pastors still try to preach 8-track sermons, unwilling to recognize that today's younger people understand the world in a manner different from any other generation before. Unfortunately, it's all too easy to ignore the problem and shift the blame by suggesting that many listeners just aren't committed to spiritual growth.

The irony is that people today, more than at any other time in history, are seeking to understand God's Word at a deeper level. However, they want to do more than just listen to it—they want to actively participate in it.

As a result, cutting-edge ministers and speakers are beginning to recognize the importance of incorporating elements of active and interactive learning into their sermons. The best way to learn something is through experience. And why should God's Word be any different? In a real sense, *Bore No More!* and *Bore No More! 2* were written in direct response to that question. While there is no denying that the Holy Spirit is an integral part of people's understanding of God's Word, on a human level, individuals still learn and process God's Word as they do anything else.

Bore No More! 2 provides the necessary resources to incorporate participatory and experiential learning into a sermon. The creative ideas aren't meant to replace a sermon, just to help illustrate it. As you begin to incorporate some of them into your preaching, you'll notice that your sermon will change from a teaching experience into a learning experience.

If you're just beginning to incorporate activities that promote active and interactive participation from your congregation, you might want to check the risk rating provided with each idea. A low risk rating indicates a lower level of participation from the congregation. A high-risk activity may actually require the participants to get out of their seats and move around. If your congregation has little experience with this type sermon, start off slowly and build toward greater participation and acceptance. Remember, risk-taking has always been a vital element of the Christian faith. As Robert Nash aptly puts it, "A church that fails to risk fails at the single most essential task of the church."

As you peruse the pages of this book, you'll also discover just how easy *Bore No More! 2* is to use. Each activity is simple to do, and each requires only minimal preparation. For quick reference, a Scripture index, a topical index, and a risk-rating index have been provided. For ministers who follow the lectionary, a variety of biblical passages from Year A and Year B have been included.

So if you've discovered that your listeners aren't retaining much from your sermons these days, don't blame yourself, and don't blame the congregation. Just turn the pages of this book, make a selection from among all the great activities, and incorporate it into your sermon this week. Your congregation will be engaged, and you'll be surprised at how well it works. Best yet, neither you nor your congregation will ever be the same.

A House of Blocks

TOPIC: GOD'S FOUNDATION

SCRIPTURE: MATTHEW 7:24-29

Use this idea to remind participants of the importance of building their lives on a solid foundation. For this activity you'll need a set of children's blocks to build a tower.

Throughout the sermon, reinforce each point by stacking a block in a tower so that the congregation can observe the developing structure. Make sure that the stand you use is easily movable— a small table or an audiovisual cart would work well. Carefully place each block so that the tower appears to be strong and evenly balanced. As you build it, verbally draw attention to the strength that is developing through the balanced placement of each block.

At the appropriate point in your service, pick up or quickly tip your stand so that the blocks fall over. Say: **No matter how carefully constructed and well balanced a structure appears, it is the stability of the foundation that makes the difference. Balance in our lives is healthy and important, but it can never take the place of the firm foundation found only in Christ.**

Nail-Pierced Hands

TOPIC: SIN

SCRIPTURE: MATTHEW 27:11-54

VIEW FROM THE PEW

I like sermons that...bring the Bible to life.

This powerful and intense reflective experience truly links us to Christ through his sufferings. You'll need a large wooden cross, a hammer, and nails for this active illustration. Stand the cross on the floor at the back of one of the aisles in your worship area. Place the hammer next to it.

As you encourage your worshipers to prepare their hearts for the Lord's Supper, ask them to think of the sinful lives God has called them from. Have your ushers distribute a nail to each person. Say: **These nails represent the depth of Christ's sacrifice for each of our sins.** Encourage the participants to consider their own sinful lives by spending a few moments in quiet meditation.

After a few moments, ask the congregation to proceed to the cross and drive the nails into it. Then, to symbolize God's ultimate forgiveness through Christ, have each person walk to the front of the worship area to receive the elements of the Lord's Supper.

(Note: Make sure that you have a plan for helping those who cannot move around easily. You might ask ushers or other identified participants to take immobile individuals' nails to the cross on their behalf and serve them the Lord's Supper at their seats.)

Bewildered and Amazed

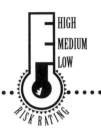

HIGH
MEDIUM
LOW

RISK RATING

TOPIC: THE RESURRECTION
SCRIPTURE: MARK 16:1-8

This activity illustrates that the reality of God's plan for creation often goes far beyond the logic of our finite and rational minds.

"Amazed," "perplexed," and "bewildered" are just a few words that describe the emotions of the women who went to the tomb to anoint Jesus' body only to discover he was not there. Today the Resurrection remains one of God's most astonishing miracles.

Either before your message or at another appropriate time, have ushers hand out enough watermelon seeds for everyone to have one. (These seeds are easily obtainable during springtime at lawn and garden supply stores.)

When the seeds have been distributed, ask all those who have ever raised watermelons to raise their hands. Next, ask if anyone knows the average weight of a full-grown watermelon (approximately fifteen to thirty pounds).

Say: **For a moment, let us consider the amazing, perplexing, and irrational story of a watermelon seed. How is it that with any logical stretch of the mind, we might imagine that God can grow this seed into a ripe, juicy watermelon, inlaid again with many more seeds, each capable of growing into thirty-pound watermelons?**

Ask the congregation to form groups of three to discuss the following questions:

● **What is the most amazing aspect of the miracle of a watermelon seed?**

● **What is the most amazing aspect of the Resurrection story?**

After allowing groups a few minutes for discussion, ask them to assign one of the following characters to each member:

● Mary, mother of Jesus
● Peter
● a guard at the tomb

Have them take a moment to imagine what must have been going through their characters' minds at the moment they discovered or

VIEW FROM THE PEW

I like sermons that... make Scripture come alive and communicate it in a relevant, modern-day style.

heard that Jesus was no longer in the tomb. Next, ask them each to share their thoughts and reflections with the others in their groups.

Conclude the small-group discussion by having participants share with their groups what makes the Resurrection story real for them.

After a few more minutes of discussion, ask for a few volunteers to share their thoughts with the whole congregation.

Continue your message, stressing that although to a rational mind the Resurrection story indeed sounds amazing and even perplexing, nothing is beyond God's power.

Reprinted from *Climbing the Church Walls* by Rob Portlock. © 1991 by Rob Portlock. Used by permission of InterVarsity Press, P.O. Box 1400, Downers Grove, IL 60515.

Put Your Faith on the Mat

TOPIC: YOUR FAITH WILL SAVE YOU

SCRIPTURE: MARK 2:1-12

Use this activity to illustrate that God honors the faith of his children. You will need a stretcher or a mat similar to the one described in the Bible passage. Each participant must also have access to a pen or pencil and a blank note card.

After you have read Mark 2:1-12, say: **Does God respond any differently to our faith than he did to the faith described in this passage? Not only was this man healed, but his sins were forgiven and he was given the gift of eternal life. God responds to the faith of his children. On your note card, write a prayer concern, knowing that God will answer it. Express your faith by bringing the card forward and placing it on the mat** [or stretcher].

After the participants have had an opportunity to respond, pray over their requests.

I don't like sermons that...don't have enough illustrations; I'm a visual-learning person.

HIGH
MEDIUM
LOW

RISK RATING

A Time to Share

TOPIC: GOD'S PRESENCE

SCRIPTURE: ECCLESIASTES 3:1-13

VIEW FROM THE PEW

A sermon that is memorable to me...draws on a vivid illustration.

This experience helps people of all generations get to know one another on a more intimate level.

After reading Ecclesiastes 3:1-13 aloud, form groups of five. Explain that participants can't be related to more than one other person in their groups and that at least three generations must be represented in each group.

Allow a minute or two for groups to assemble. Say: **Ecclesiastes 3:1-13 tells us that every life event has its appropriate season. Share with others in your group the season of life you are in right now. Is it a time to weep? a time to laugh? a time to keep? a time to throw away? a time to be silent or a time to speak? Be sure to explain why you're in that season.**

Give everyone adequate time to share, and then say: **The passage in Ecclesiastes makes it clear that no matter what season we're in, God is in control of our lives. Discuss how God is present in your life right now.**

After everyone has had a few minutes to share, allow participants to return to their original seats. Continue your sermon, encouraging everyone to be aware of God's presence in every circumstance.

"YOU BETTER DO AS THE SIGN SAYS. PASTOR SPIFFNER'S SERMONS TEND TO BE A BIT ON THE LIVELY SIDE."

My Choice

TOPIC: CHOOSING JESUS

SCRIPTURE: MATTHEW 25:31-46

Use this idea to emphasize that our choices regarding Christ are eternal.

At the appropriate time during your sermon, ask participants to stand and move as close to the center of the room as possible. If you have a center aisle, have as many people as possible stand in the aisle.

Say: **I'm going to present some choices and will ask you to choose one option or the other. If you choose the first option, move to the side of the room to my left. If you choose the second option, move to the right side of the room. After you have responded to the first question, I will ask you to return to the center and respond to another one. There are five questions altogether.**

After everyone is in place, present the following choices. Remind people each time which direction they are to move.

- **Would you rather live by the beach or the mountains?**
- **Do you prefer dogs or cats?**
- **Would you choose to spend the day in the city or the night in the country?**
- **Would you rather make yourself smarter or better looking?**
- **Would you rather be five minutes late or five minutes early?**

After the participants have returned to their seats, read Matthew 25:31-46. Say: **Your choices in this activity determined what side of the room you ended up on. In much the same way, during your life on earth, you have a choice to make that can determine where you'll spend eternity.** Continue your sermon, encouraging the congregation to choose Jesus.

Mary's Miracle

TOPIC: JESUS' BIRTH

SCRIPTURE: LUKE 1:26-38

I like sermons that...are challenging, that give me something to think about.

This activity will help your congregation understand and celebrate the miracle of Jesus' birth.

Before the service, place a photocopy of the "Readers Theater" handout (p. 19-20) on every seat or in your church bulletin. Ask a woman and a man who are comfortable reading aloud in front of people to participate in this activity. Assign the woman to play the part of Mary and the man to play the part of Gabriel. At the appropriate time for the activity to begin, ask them to stand at the front of the room with you.

Read Luke 1:26-38, and ask the congregation to refer to the handout. Say: **We're going to read the Scripture passage from Luke again. This time, however, everyone will participate. We'll also include other Scripture passages that shed light on the miracle.**

Assign one section of your congregation to be group 1, one section to be group 2, and the other to be group 3. Explain that you will read the leader's parts and members of the congregation will read the parts designated for their groups. Point out that one portion of the reading will be read by all the women in the congregation and that the final portion will be read aloud by the entire congregation.

When everyone is ready, begin reading. At the conclusion of the readers theater, continue your sermon. You may want to emphasize the prophecies as well as the anticipation that led up to the miraculous event described in Luke 1:26-38.

READERS THEATER

Leader: "In the sixth month, God sent the angel Gabriel to Nazareth, a town in Galilee, to a virgin pledged to be married to a man named Joseph, a descendant of David. The virgin's name was Mary."

Group 1: "The angel went to her and said, 'Greetings, you who are highly favored! The Lord is with you.' "

Group 2: "Mary was greatly troubled at his words and wondered what kind of greeting this might be."

Mary: Wow! This is weird!

Group 3: "But the angel said to her, 'Do not be afraid, Mary, you have found favor with God.' "

Gabriel: Don't worry—this is good news!

Group 1: " 'You will be with child and give birth to a son, and you are to give him the name Jesus.' "

Leader: "Therefore the Lord himself will give you a sign: The virgin will be with child and will give birth to a son, and will call him Immanuel."

Group 2: " 'He will be great and will be called the Son of the Most High. The Lord God will give him the throne of his father David.' "

Leader: "A shoot will come up from the stump of Jesse; from his roots a Branch will bear fruit."

Group 3: " 'And he will reign over the house of Jacob forever; his kingdom will never end.' "

Leader: "All this took place to fulfill what the Lord had said through the prophet: 'The virgin will be with child and will give birth to a son, and they will call him Immanuel'—which means, 'God with us.' "

All Women: " 'How will this be,' Mary asked the angel, 'since I am a virgin?' "

Mary: Wow! This is even more weird!

Group 1: "The angel answered, 'The Holy Spirit will come upon you, and the power of the Most High will overshadow you. So the holy one to be born will be called the Son of God.' "

Gabriel: Don't worry—God has a plan!

Group 2: " 'Even Elizabeth your relative is going to have a child in her old age, and she who was said to be barren is in her sixth month.' "

Group 3: " 'For nothing is impossible with God.' "

Leader: "But you, Bethlehem Ephrathah, though you are small among the clans of Judah, out of you will come for me one who will be ruler over Israel, whose origins are from of old, from ancient times."

Group 1: " 'I am the Lord's servant,' Mary answered. 'May it be to me as you have said.' "

Mary: I'll trust in God's plan.

Group 2: "Then the angel left her."

Gabriel: Gotta go.

Group 3: "But the angel said to them, 'Do not be afraid. I bring you good news of great joy that will be for all the people. Today in the town of David a Savior has been born to you; he is Christ the Lord. This will be a sign to you: You will find a baby wrapped in cloths and lying in a manger.' Suddenly a great company of the heavenly host appeared with the angel, praising God and saying, 'Glory to God in the highest, and on earth peace to men on whom his favor rests.' "

All: "For to us a child is born, to us a son is given, and the government will be on his shoulders. And he will be called Wonderful Counselor, Mighty God, Everlasting Father, Prince of Peace. Of the increase of his government and peace there will be no end. He will reign on David's throne and over his kingdom, establishing and upholding it with justice and righteousness from that time on and forever. The zeal of the Lord Almighty will accomplish this."

Powerful Stories

HIGH
MEDIUM
LOW

RISK RATING

TOPIC: PENTECOST

SCRIPTURE: ACTS 2:1-21

This idea will help bring the story of Pentecost alive for your congregation.

Before the service, place paper and a pen or pencil at every seat. After reading Acts 2:1-21 during your sermon, say: **Please take a few minutes to think about what this experience may have been like for someone who witnessed it. Think about that experience from the perspective of a specific character—either someone who is mentioned in the biblical account or someone who isn't. For example, maybe you want to think about what it might have been like to be a small child in the crowd. Or perhaps you'd like to think about the experience from the perspective of a visitor from another country.**

After you've thought about what the experience might have been like for your specific character, take a few moments to write a retelling of that experience from that character's perspective.

Give participants several minutes to write. When they have had adequate time, ask for volunteers to stand, describe their perspectives, and read their stories. You may want to have the readers come forward so they can be heard and seen by everyone. Or you may want to have a few microphones available throughout the room.

When the volunteers are finished, continue your sermon. Emphasize the amazing events of Pentecost and the power of the Holy Spirit in the lives of Christians today.

VIEW FROM THE PEW

What makes a sermon memorable to you?...One that causes me to become excited!

My Offering

TOPIC: GOD'S STRENGTH

SCRIPTURE: 2 CORINTHIANS 12:2-10

Use this idea to help members of the congregation understand that God's strength must shine through their weaknesses.

Before the service, place an index card and a pen or pencil on every seat. After discussing 2 Corinthians 12:2-10 in your sermon, say: **Let's take time right now to think about our personal weaknesses. Answer this question for yourself: What is something you perceive as a personal weakness that God might use to demonstrate his glory? For example, maybe you're shy, and it's difficult for you to reach out to other people. But if you were to rely on God, he may choose to show his glory through you by giving you the strength to reach out to other shy people. Or maybe you have an illness that God is waiting to use to reach out to someone else in your situation.**

Give the participants several moments to consider their responses, and then continue: **Most of the time, we think of these weaknesses as afflictions that hinder us. It is important to consider, however, that they might be something God has given us as a way of demonstrating his glory in our lives.**

Instruct everyone to write a description of his or her weakness on an index card. Just below the description, have each participant write one way he or she sees the potential for God to demonstrate his glory through that weakness.

When everyone has finished, say: **At this time, I'd like you to make a commitment to God. We're going to take an offering. If you're ready to commit your weakness to the glory of God, drop your card in the offering plate to demonstrate your commitment. If you're not ready to take that step, hold on to your card and pray during the week that God will show you how to turn your weakness into his strength.**

After the ushers have received the offering of index cards, continue your sermon.

East vs. West

HIGH
MEDIUM
LOW

RISK RATING

TOPIC: SERMON REVIEW

SCRIPTURE: ANY

This activity is a fun way to review key points of a sermon (or a series of sermons). Before the service, place a whiteboard in the middle of the platform and ask someone to dress up as a referee to help you. Write at least ten questions you want to ask the congregation about the sermon (or series).

When you are ready for the review activity to begin, form two groups: the East and the West. If possible, place two to three people in the congregation with hand-held microphones. Announce that you are going to play the East vs. West game. The rules are as follows:

● Teams win points for correct answers.

● Teams lose points for incorrect answers.

● Teams can gain points for sportsmanlike conduct such as cheering loudly for the other team when it is successful.

● Teams can lose points for unsportsmanlike conduct, such as arguing with the moderator.

Proceed to ask the questions as if you were the moderator of a game show. After asking each question, call on the first person to stand up and raise his or her hand. If that individual answers correctly, award points to his or her team. If the other team responds appropriately (by cheering, for example), award that team points as well. Make this review game as crazy as you want it to be. Your congregation will love it!

Cleansed

TOPIC: FORGIVENESS

SCRIPTURE: PSALM 51:1-7

Use this idea to cement the concept that Christians are cleansed from sin by Jesus' sacrifice on the cross. Before the sermon, set up a dry-erase whiteboard at the front of the church. You'll also need a dark permanent marker (not black because of racial overtones), a red dry-erase marker, and an eraser for the whiteboard. You might want to try the illustration ahead of time to ensure it will work with the particular markers you have.

After you've talked about David's sin and his plea for cleansing through forgiveness in Psalm 51:1-7, describe how our cleansing from sin comes through Jesus' blood on the cross. Hold up the dark permanent marker, and say: **This permanent marker represents sin. It's not supposed to be used on a whiteboard like this one.**

Ask a volunteer to join you. Have the individual confirm that the marker is a permanent one. Next, ask the volunteer to write the word "sin" in big, bold, capital letters on the whiteboard. Then thank and dismiss the helper. Say: **Like David, we've all sinned. As far as we're concerned, that sin is on our permanent record in permanent ink like this marker.**

Have another volunteer come to the front, take the eraser, and demonstrate that the dark ink won't erase. As you dismiss that person, say: **We have no way to erase sin from our lives. And that sin separates us from God. However, in his great love and compassion, God sent Jesus to die on the cross, bearing our sins. This red marker will represent Jesus' blood that covers our sins.**

Have a third volunteer use the red dry-erase marker to quickly cover every bit of the dark marker on the whiteboard. Dismiss the volunteer and say: **Since our sins are covered by Jesus' sacrifice, if we seek forgiveness as David did, God cleanses us from all our sin.**

Call a fourth volunteer forward, and ask the person to erase the board. (Everything on the board will be erased, including the permanent marker.) As the board is erased, read or quote from the Psalm 51 passage, saying: **"Wash away all my iniquity and**

What I like least about sermons is...ideas that are hard to follow.

24

cleanse me from my sin...wash me, and I will be whiter than snow."

Continue your sermon by challenging the participants to seek the forgiveness and cleansing God offers through Jesus' sacrifice.

"No, Pastor Smith, it's 'Spring forward, fall back!'"

A Great Deal

TOPIC: FOLLOWING JESUS
SCRIPTURE: MATTHEW 16:21-28

Use this idea to introduce the idea of giving up something of lesser value to gain something of greater value.

You'll need a ten-dollar bill. Begin the illustration by saying: **I need one volunteer to give me a five-dollar bill. This is not for the offering, and I will not be giving the five dollars back to you. Who will give me a five-dollar bill?**

Wait for a volunteer to approach you with a five-dollar bill. (If no one responds, lower the amount to one dollar.) Take the bill, and thank the person with a smile. Act happy to have the money, and then put the bill in your pocket. As the person starts to leave, say: **Wait! I said I wouldn't give your five dollars back, but I didn't say I wouldn't give you something better.** Pull out the ten-dollar bill, show everyone what it is, and give it to the volunteer. Say: **Here's your reward for trusting me.**

Dismiss the person, and read aloud Matthew 16:21-28. Next, have each person in the congregation turn to a partner and discuss the following questions:

● **Why did you hesitate to give me five dollars?**

● **When might it be wise to voluntarily give up something of value?**

● **What does trust have to do with giving up something of value?**

● **How is this like Jesus' words, "For whoever wants to save his life will lose it, but whoever loses his life for me will find it"?**

After the discussion, have a few volunteers tell about their discussions. Continue with your sermon, emphasizing the value of giving up worldly things to gain an eternal relationship with God through Jesus.

If you want to increase the risk and the impact of this activity, ask for a ten-dollar bill and give a twenty in return. Or ask for a twenty and give a fifty!

How Great God Is!

HIGH
MEDIUM
LOW

RISK RATING

TOPIC: WORSHIP

SCRIPTURE: LUKE 1:46-55

Use this idea to help participants add depth to their worship experience. Arrange in advance for a female vocalist to sing any version of the Magnificat as spoken by Mary and recorded in Luke 1:46-55. Another option is to have an actress do a dramatic reading of the passage. You'll also need paper and pens or pencils for each participant.

After you've introduced the passage, ask congregational members to close their eyes and pretend that Mary has come to visit them to express her joy in being selected by God. As they do so, have the actress or vocalist present the Magnificat.

When the presentation is finished, have people gather into groups of three or four to discuss the following questions. (Encourage them to refer to Luke 1:46-55 as they do.)

● **How did Mary feel toward God?**

● **How do you feel about what God has done in your life?**

After groups have been allowed adequate time to discuss the questions, say: **Now I'd like each group to create a brief reading expressing its participants' feelings about the greatness of God, similar to what Mary did.**

Distribute paper and pencils. Assure the groups that the readings don't have to be complex or musical and that participants won't be forced to share them. Allow about five minutes, and then ask volunteers to share their readings as a worship offering to God.

You might want to use this activity to close your message. Or you might decide to continue your sermon, helping people better understand the purpose of worship.

VIEW FROM THE PEW

Would you like to see your pastor try some new methods other than lecture during the sermon time?... Yes! Something to capture our attention and interest.

After All He'd Done for Me

TOPIC: OBEDIENCE

SCRIPTURE: JOHN 15:9-17

Use this idea to challenge participants to be obedient to God.

After beginning your examination of John 15:9-17, say: **I'd like you all to stand up, turn and face your left, and then extend your arms straight out to your sides.** Wait until most people have appropriately responded. Then say: **While you hold your arms there, reflect silently on the questions I'm going to ask.**

Ask the following questions slowly, pausing a few seconds after each one to allow people to reflect.

VIEW FROM THE PEW

One encouraging thought I'd like to share with people who deliver sermons...your work is very important.

● **Why did you do as I suggested and extend your arms out to the side?**

● **If I asked you to get down on your hands and knees and meow like a cat, would you do it?**

● **If I had risked my life to push you out of the way of a train, would you then get down on your hands and knees and meow if I asked you to?**

● **What would I have to do to make you willing to do whatever I ask of you?**

● **Why do you continue to endure the pain of having your arms extended?**

Let people drop their arms to their sides and be seated. Then have them form groups of three or four, read John 15:9-17, and discuss this question: **In light of what Jesus endured for us, what should our response to him be?**

After a few minutes, have a few volunteers report on their discussions. Then continue with your sermon, challenging people to obey God's commands out of gratitude for Christ's sacrifice.

Passing Grade

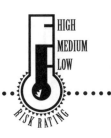

HIGH
MEDIUM
LOW

RISK RATING

TOPIC: SALVATION BY FAITH
SCRIPTURE: EPHESIANS 2:1-10

Use this idea to help participants understand the true nature of God's grace. Prior to the beginning of the worship service, prepare two kinds of report cards. Write "Report Card" on one of them, but leave the rest of it blank. Write "Report Card" on the outside of the other one, and write "A+" on the inside followed by "signed by God." Fold both cards in half. Make enough copies for each congregational member to have one of each, and be sure everyone has access to a pencil or a pen.

Say: **Let's pretend that we're all at the pearly gates, standing before God. We want to get into heaven, but God is asking for our report cards.**

At this point, quickly distribute the blank report cards, and say: **Think back on your life. If you had to give yourself an honest grade, what would it be? How well have you lived the Christian life? Write the grade you think you would deserve, then fold your report card so no one else can see it.** Give participants a minute to reflect and write their responses.

Silently take a wastebasket and the preprinted A+ report cards out into the congregation. As you approach each person, take the report card in his or her hand, and without looking at the grade, drop it into the wastebasket. Then hand the person an A+ report card. Be sure everyone receives one. (**Note:** If you have a large congregation, ask ushers to help receive the old report cards and distribute new ones.)

After everyone has looked at his or her new report card, say: **The report cards that we threw into that wastebasket would have kept us all out of heaven. We'd have been expelled from the class. How many of us deserve an A+ from God? However, the Bible makes it clear that the only grade that will get us into heaven is the A+ given by God. That is the way God's grace works!**

Continue your sermon, encouraging people to trust only in the salvation offered by grace through faith, and not in anything they have done themselves.

HIGH
MEDIUM
LOW

RISK RATING

Comfort-Zone Connections

TOPIC: CHANGE

SCRIPTURE: GENESIS 12:1-4

Use this idea to introduce a deeper understanding of the feelings Abram experienced when God asked him to leave his comfort zone in search of God's promises.

Before the sermon, ask everyone to stand. Give congregation members the option to greet others who are either

● standing near enough that they don't have to leave their pews in order to greet them,

● three rows directly in front or behind them, or

● at the opposite side of the worship area.

Have some music playing in the background while the congregation completes your instructions. After a few minutes, ask participants to sit down next to the people they went to greet.

Next, have them form groups of between four and six within their immediate area and discuss these questions:

● **How did you decide whom to greet?**

● **How would you have responded if you had not been given an option but were instructed exactly where to go and who to greet?**

After allowing approximately five minutes for discussion, have a reporter from a few of the groups share their responses.

During the sermon, relate the participants' experiences to the reasons Abram might have had for not wanting to leave his "comfort zone."

VIEW FROM THE PEW

I like sermons that...are clear, using object lessons that everyone understands—even children—and incorporate biblical characters that help us realize that they faced the same things we face.

A Command Performance

HIGH
MEDIUM
LOW

RISK RATING

TOPIC: THE TEN COMMANDMENTS

SCRIPTURE: EXODUS 20:1-17

Use this activity after a sermon about the Ten Commandments to encourage your congregation to develop a plan to put the Ten Commandments into action in their lives.

To begin, provide copies of the "Ten Commandments" handout (p. 32) to congregation members. Instruct everyone to fold the handout on the lines and tear the commandments apart. Say: **Stack the commandments in order of how difficult they are for you to keep. Put the least challenging commandment on the bottom of the stack, and continue until the most difficult one is on top.**

Allow a few moments of silence as participants commit to improve their attitudes toward the commandment that is most personally challenging to them. Invite them to use their tablets as bookmarks that will remind them to ask God for the strength to obey his commands.

VIEW FROM THE PEW

Our pastor uses a lot of current illustrations that really make it fun to be in church.

TEN COMMANDMENTS

YOU SHALL HAVE NO OTHER GODS BEFORE ME.

YOU SHALL MAKE FOR YOURSELF NO IDOLS, NOR WORSHIP THEM.

YOU SHALL NOT MISUSE THE NAME OF THE LORD.

REMEMBER THE SABBATH DAY BY KEEPING IT HOLY.

HONOR YOUR FATHER AND MOTHER.

YOU SHALL NOT MURDER.

YOU SHALL NOT COMMIT ADULTERY.

YOU SHALL NOT STEAL.

YOU SHALL NOT GIVE FALSE TESTIMONY.

YOU SHALL NOT COVET YOUR NEIGHBOR'S PROPERTY.

Clean Mouth, Fresh Breath

HIGH
MEDIUM
LOW

RISK RATING

TOPIC: GOD'S HOLINESS

SCRIPTURE: ISAIAH 6:1-8

This activity illustrates that there is no substitute for God's cleansing touch. Before worship begins, prepare the items needed to brush your teeth. Plan to have a glass of fresh water and a basin to complete the process in front of the congregation. You will also need individually wrapped pieces of sugarless gum for your congregation.

Talk about how, as a pastor, you have realized the importance of having fresh breath while interacting with the members of your congregation to bring the Word of God to them. You might explain that you didn't brush your teeth this morning but you simply couldn't bring yourself to preach God's Word without brushing your teeth. Quickly brush your teeth. Stress how much better you feel with fresh breath.

Say: **Some reports tell us that dentists recommend chewing sugarless gum when we can't brush because sugarless gum removes plaque and cleanses our breath. So just in case some of you would like that freshly brushed feeling, I brought sugarless gum for all of you.** Have the ushers assist in distributing the gum, and as the congregation begins to chew it, say:

Before this experience I was identifying with the prophet Isaiah, who said, "I am a man of unclean lips, and I live among a people of unclean lips." Isaiah knew he was standing on God's holy ground with a message from God himself. His guilt in the presence of God's holiness was nearly unbearable. Isaiah was clearly speaking of a problem more serious than one that would be solved merely by brushing his teeth. In the same way, we must take our own sinful natures very seriously, as if we, too, were standing on God's holy ground.

Throughout the sermon, weave in the concept that God provided for Isaiah's cleansing. God cleansed not only Isaiah's mouth, but also his sin and guilt. There is no substitute or "next best thing" to God's cleansing touch—no sugarless-gum experience, only a personal encounter with the holy, living God.

Gratitudes

TOPIC: THE BEATITUDES
SCRIPTURE: MATTHEW 5:1-12

This activity will help the congregation better understand the Beatitudes.

Before worship, prepare a poster-sized copy of each Beatitude and a transparency of verse 12a: "Rejoice and be glad, because great is your reward in heaven." Designate the verse number on each poster. Enlist the help of nine volunteers to act as group leaders during this experience. You will also need a marker for each group.

At the appropriate time, have your group leaders go to separate areas and hold up their posters so that everyone will know where each group is to meet. (**Note:** A large congregation may wish to have two groups for each Beatitude.)

Say: **Think about a life experience that clearly demonstrates a particular Beatitude. The experience doesn't necessarily have to be a personal one; it can involve another person or a story that you've heard. Proceed to the particular Beatitude that best represents this story.** Allow time for all the participants to share the stories with their groups.

After an appropriate interval, ask groups to paraphrase their Beatitudes in light of their discussions and then record the paraphrases on the back side of their posters.

When groups have finished, have each group hang its poster near the front of the church. Next, have each group read its paraphrase in unison to the congregation. After all the groups have done this, have the entire congregation read Matthew 5:12a together.

During the remainder of your sermon, you may want to refer to some of the wisdom gleaned from the group discussions to help the congregation better understand the Beatitudes.

Work for Hire

RISK RATING

TOPIC: GOD'S GENEROSITY

SCRIPTURE: MATTHEW 20:1-16

As a good introduction to your sermon, try this idea to help the congregation understand that God's generosity is not dependent on our performance. You'll need six uninhibited volunteers to help and a one-dollar bill in an envelope for each of them.

Ask the volunteers to stand in a line near you. Say: **I'd like you to help me remind everyone here today of the old camp song "Father Abraham." We don't really have time for the whole song, so I'm going to ask each of you to participate in only one verse. As soon as I give you the verse, please begin doing the motions, and continue doing them until I ask you to stop. This is not a gratis job. I will reward each of you for your participation.**

Begin by assigning the final verse to your most energetic volunteer. It requires the volunteer to perform the following motions simultaneously: move the right arm, left arm, right leg, left leg; lift chin up; and turn around. For each of the remaining volunteers, remove a motion until the final person has only to move his or her right arm. After singing through one verse of the song, reward the volunteers. (Obviously, the one assigned the most movements will have worked harder than the others and will be somewhat tired after the verse.)

Hand out the envelopes, and ask the last volunteer to open his or her envelope. Make an issue of how much effort each individual's contribution required. Make it sound as though the first volunteer, who did the most work, really deserves a substantial reward. Have the others open their envelopes one at a time. Show equal enthusiasm for the one-dollar reward given to each volunteer.

Continue your sermon, and reflect on any congregational responses to the seemingly unfair reward.

After reading the Scripture passage, say: **This activity created a parallel experience to the parable presented in the Scripture reading. The reward was not something the volunteers were entitled to, for they all *volunteered* to help. Instead, it was the result of generosity. In the same way, God's rewards are not an entitlement or an earned benefit but simply the result of his abundant generosity.**

VIEW FROM THE PEW

I don't like sermons that...are boring.

HIGH
MEDIUM
LOW

RISK RATING

Throw It Down

TOPIC: PALM SUNDAY

SCRIPTURE: MARK 11:1-11

VIEW FROM THE PEW

What makes a sermon memorable to you?...One that uses illustrations and object lessons.

This activity will help your congregation get a better idea of what it was like to stand on the road as Jesus rode into Jerusalem on what is now called Palm Sunday.

After you've discussed the Scripture passage, encourage your congregation members to stand along the center aisle with their belongings in hand. Have them close their eyes and imagine they are lining the streets of Jerusalem.

Say: **The people of Jerusalem were from all stations of life, much like people today. These people enthusiastically lined the streets with their possessions to celebrate the coming Messiah. For some of them, it possibly would have meant risking the destruction of their only coats. Yet these people threw what they had into the street to honor their coming King.**

Ask members of the congregation to take a similar risk—to shout "Hosanna!" and to choose a belonging in their possession to cast into the aisle as a symbol of their joy for the coming Messiah.

As the musicians play their instruments softly or the choir sings quietly, ask participants to consider what it must have been like to see Jesus pass by that day as you dramatically read Mark 11:7-10.

Another option is to have someone play the part of Jesus, dress in a white robe, and walk down the aisle during the dramatic Scripture reading.

Paid in Full

HIGH
MEDIUM
LOW

RISK RATING

TOPIC: ACCOUNTABILITY

SCRIPTURE: ROMANS 14:1-12

This activity will help members of your congregation examine their priorities and discover if their daily activities are bringing honor to God. During your message, tie in the concept of using an appointment calendar.

Say: **An appointment calendar usually becomes a record of events. Each record is unique and personal. It is usually sketchy and consists of a word or phrase written down as a reminder. To look at someone else's calendar is to get an incomplete picture of what actually happened. The same is true when we examine someone else's life. We get only an incomplete picture. We don't understand the motives or the circumstances of a given event. The only person whose calendar we can fully interpret is our own.**

Ask participants to take out their appointment calendars if they have them on their person and to think about all the events recorded on them for the past week. Have everyone reflect on how those events connect to their lives as Christians. Did the events honor God? Did they provide an opportunity to love in Jesus' name? Were there events they would rather not bring before God? How do they think God would evaluate their calendars?

As part of this activity, offer opportunities for both confessing sins to God and dedicating the weeks ahead to serving God more fully.

HIGH
MEDIUM
LOW

RISK RATING

Faith Headlines

TOPIC: FAITH

SCRIPTURE: 2 CORINTHIANS 5:6-10

Use this activity to help the congregation remember that Christians are called to a life of trust and faith.

Prior to the service, gather current headlines from newspapers or magazines that reflect the darkness of the world around us. Use the headlines to create a responsive reading. Print them either on a handout or a transparency, or simply read them to the congregation. After each headline, have the congregation say in unison, "We live by faith, not by sight" (2 Corinthians 5:7). At the end of the reading, read verse 9 together: "So, we make it our goal to please [God], whether we are at home in the body or away from it."

Your reading might sound like this:

● Bomb Explodes in Northern Ireland, Killing Two

We live by faith, not by sight.

● Newborn Found Abandoned in Downtown Dumpster

We live by faith, not by sight.

● Mounting Evidence of Corruption in Mayor's Office

We live by faith, not by sight.

● Two Million Dollars of Confiscated Cocaine Missing

We live by faith, not by sight. So we make it our goal to please [God], whether we are at home in the body, or away from it (2 Corinthians 5:9).

Worry Less, Pray More

HIGH
MEDIUM
LOW

RISK RATING

TOPIC: TRUSTING GOD

SCRIPTURE: PHILIPPIANS 4:4-7

This activity will encourage the participants to be sensitive to the needs of those around them and to pray for one another.

Following the sermon, ask congregation members each to pair up with someone they have not yet spoken to today. Ask the participants to move from their seats and choose a neutral spot in which to be seated together.

Ask members of each pair to share the following:

● a situation that has recently jeopardized their ability to have a positive worship experience,

● a new perspective on the situation after today's message, and

● an encouraging prayer for their partner's situation.

After an appropriate interval, have the partners take each other's hands and repeat, after you, this personalized promise from Philippians 4:7:

"And the peace of God,
Which transcends all understanding,
Will guard your heart and your mind
In Christ Jesus."

Look to the Light

TOPIC: GOD'S LEADERSHIP

SCRIPTURE: EXODUS 14:10-31

Use this visual illusion to help your congregation recognize that we can choose to focus on God rather than the darkness of our circumstances. Reproduce the "Look to the Light" handout (p. 42) so that it fits within your worship folder or bulletin.

After you've talked about the Hebrews' frightened response to the approach of Pharaoh's army, ask members of the congregation to hold their handouts vertically and look at the first box.

Say: **Moses led the Hebrews out of the box of slavery in Egypt. But they complained that at least in Egypt they knew their box contained a home and a bed to lie on.**

Instruct the congregation to look at the second box. Say: **Now they found themselves in a predicament with no visible way out. They felt small and insignificant. Their eyes weren't really focused on anything but their own insignificance in the face of Pharaoh's army. They seemed to be surrounded by darkness.**

Have the congregation look at the third box. Say: **Their opinion of God was no better. He was a God in a box of their own creation. Worse yet, he was a God who had left them hanging on a hook of empty promises.**

Have the congregation fold the paper on the lines accordion style so that the boxes are joined together (demonstrate if necessary). Say: **All the Hebrews perceived was darkness around them. But God was ready to turn their world around that day.**

Instruct the participants to turn their papers one-quarter turn to the right (horizontally). Say: **They were so caught up in the darkness of their limitations that they failed to look at the light.**

Instead of looking at the dark color of the boxes, look at the white, and you will see exactly what the Hebrews saw when the Red Sea parted. God was in the midst of their situation. They had only to choose to look at him. They had only to focus on the light rather than the darkness. They had only to focus on God rather than their own circumstances.

Continue your sermon, encouraging your listeners to focus on God in the darkness of whatever situations they may face in the upcoming week.

LOOK TO THE LIGHT

This side up

1.

- -

2.

- -

3.

Write It on Your Heart

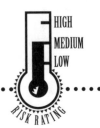

TOPIC: GOD'S COMMANDMENTS

SCRIPTURE: DEUTERONOMY 11:18-21

This activity will remind the participants to fix God's words in their hearts and minds. Use adding-machine tape, or cut strips of paper into streamers. Write "Love the Lord your God" in 2½-inch letters on each streamer. You will need enough strips for each participant to receive one as well as a few extras. (The strips handed out to the participants could be smaller, 1X5 inches, for example.) Affix the extra streamers to door frames and window ledges and across the front of your preaching area—wherever they will be noticeable! At the beginning of your sermon, ask the congregation:

Have you noticed the message of the day? Ask participants to close their eyes and repeat the message in unison.

At the end of your sermon, ask for help distributing the message strips to everyone in the congregation. Instruct participants to roll or fold their strips and place them under their rings or watchbands, much as the Hebrews were instructed to bind the commandments to their foreheads and hands.

Say: **I challenge you to keep the paper tucked beneath your ring or watchband until someone asks you to explain what it is about. Use the opportunity to do as the Scriptures instruct: "Teach them to your children" and "talk about them when you sit at home and when you walk along the road."**

What I like best about sermons is...good illustrations that are easy to remember and emphasize the point well.

Plant Where You Can Bloom

TOPIC: PRINCIPLES OF SUCCESS

SCRIPTURE: PSALM 1

This activity will help the participants better understand that we must ground ourselves in Christ in order to yield an abundance of fruit.

Before worship begins, choose five volunteers to help with this illustration. Give each of them a small plant from a six-pack of nursery starts. (Put each plant in a paper cup if it isn't in its own container.)

Have the volunteers come forward with their plants. Read aloud the potting instructions that came with the plants. Then say: **Jesus often put a twist on the common sayings of his day. He said things like "You have heard that it was said, 'Love your neighbor and hate your enemy.' But I tell you: Love your enemies and pray for those who persecute you." Today, I have a twist for you—"You have heard that it was said 'Bloom where you're planted.' But I say: Plant where you can bloom."**

Ask the congregation to list the things the plants will need to have a successful life.

Instruct the volunteers to plant their plants in good soil. Ask for their promise to care for them according to the congregation's list of elements necessary to the plants' success. The twist becomes evident as you tell one of the volunteers to water his or her plant with water; another, cooking oil; another, ammonia; another, liquid soap; and another, coffee. After you have made the assignments, have the volunteers project how long they expect their plants to live.

Say: **Each of these plants started out with an equal opportunity to survive. What will effect them most is not the quality of care they receive, but the quality of what they are fed. We are all like plants in this way. If we "walk in the counsel of the wicked" or "stand in the way of sinners" or "sit in the seat of mockers," we will not yield much fruit. However, those who meditate on God's law day and night will yield an abundance of fruit. Although we cannot always choose our surroundings, we can choose the quality of what we are fed.**

Bare Footage

TOPIC: BRINGING GOOD NEWS
SCRIPTURE: ISAIAH 52:7-10

This activity, which focuses on the beauty of God's people, will require some planning, but it is well worth the effort as a way to begin or end your sermon.

Using either videotape or still slides, collect shots of the bare feet of selected volunteers from all age groups, followed by shots of their smiling faces. While this can be accomplished during a Sunday photo shoot, it will be more effective to take pictures of congregation members in their workplaces or school settings.

Just before showing the video or slides during the worship service, say: **Isaiah said, "How beautiful on the mountains are the feet of those who bring good news, who proclaim peace, who bring good tidings, who proclaim salvation, who say to Zion, 'Your God reigns!'** (Isaiah 52:7).

Show the video or slides as the congregation sings "Our God Reigns."

"WELCOME!"

A Little Sharing

TOPIC: MIRACLES

SCRIPTURE: JOHN 6:1-21

VIEW FROM THE PEW

Would you like to see your pastor try some new methods other than lecture during the sermon?...Yes! Something that captures our attention and interest.

This activity will remind members of your congregation not to underestimate the work of God in their lives.

You'll need a dinner roll or a loaf of French bread to share with worshippers to help them realize that God's miracles surpass all human understanding. Make sure that the size of the loaf you use corresponds to the size of your congregation. A small roll will be enough for congregations of fewer than one hundred, and a full loaf will be enough for a congregation of one thousand.

Begin by asking for a show of hands of those who believe you are holding enough bread for everyone in the congregation to have a piece. Then distribute a chunk of bread to one person in every row. Tell people that as they pass the bread along the row, the object is for each person to take a piece but also to make sure the next person will receive a piece as well. Have the ushers pick up the leftovers at the end of each aisle.

Say: **What we have just witnessed is amazing, but not a miracle. A true miracle is what the crowd of five thousand witnessed on the hillside by the Sea of Galilee. Too often we limit our faith by making assumptions about what is or is not possible. Don't let your estimates of what God can or can't do keep you from trusting him.**

As an appropriate end to this activity, ask members of the congregation to silently meditate on something they believe God is challenging them to do—something that would be impossible if not for his grace.

Doors of Foolishness

HIGH
MEDIUM
LOW

RISK RATING

TOPIC: ETERNAL LIFE

SCRIPTURE: 1 CORINTHIANS 1:18-31

This activity will demonstrate that the message of the Cross is not as foolish as it may appear.

You will need a sheet of paper and a pair of scissors for this object lesson. As you introduce your sermon, show the congregation a plain piece of paper. Say: **If I were to begin the message today by telling you that the only way to eternal life was to walk through this paper, you would consider it foolishness, no matter how much you respect me. The message of the Cross seemed nearly as foolish to the people of Corinth. The idea violated both their sensibilities and their logic.**

Proceed with the remainder of the sermon. At its conclusion, begin cutting the paper as shown in the illustration. You may want to practice this before the service or substitute a piece of paper that has already been partially cut.

Continue cutting until the paper will open into a large rectangle. Say: **What seemed like foolishness at the beginning of my message is now a very real possibility. It is, in fact, possible to walk through this piece of paper. But it is not the door to eternal life. Jesus Christ is the door. And the plan that seemed foolish to the Corinthians was not the impossible, illogical argument of a man named Paul. It was the plan of God for the salvation of humankind. It still is today, and it always will be.**

You may choose to ask two volunteers to hold this paper door as you invite the other congregation members to walk through it as a declaration of their commitment to the "foolishness" of God.

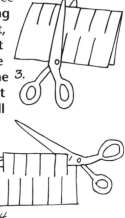

1.

2.

3.

4.

5.

It Takes Only a Spark

TOPIC: ENCOURAGEMENT

SCRIPTURE: HEBREWS 10:16-25

This activity can be used to celebrate the new life Christians have been given in Christ. For each member of the congregation, you will need a candle with a wax catcher made from a piece of aluminum foil. You will also need a single match to start the process.

After your message, say: **We have been given several privileges because of our new lives in Christ. One of the most significant is personal access to God through Christ. We often experience this access through worship. Of course, another privilege of new life is enjoying encouragement from one another. Worship is an opportunity to encourage one another to love and serve the Lord.**

Distribute the candles; then lower the lights as much as possible.

Choose a traditional blessing such as "Go in peace to love and serve the Lord" or "Let your light so shine before men that they may see your good works and glorify your father in heaven." Say these words as you light a single candle of encouragement. As each individual candle is lit, have the participant giving the light recite the same blessing. Then pray this prayer of benediction:

Father, we lift these candles to you. May we be encouraged by the light around us as it reminds us of our new lives in Christ. By this new life, may we be warmth to the chilled hearts in our world. May our good works light up the eyes of the discouraged and penetrate the walls of the isolated. May we be good stewards of the encouragement we have received through fellowship with one another. As we extinguish these flames, may your love continue to burn even more brightly in our lives. In Jesus' name, amen.

A Table Before Me

HIGH
MEDIUM
LOW

RISK RATING

TOPIC: GOD'S LOVE AND GOODNESS

SCRIPTURE: PSALM 23

This activity will remind your listeners of God's lavish hospitality and abundant protection even in the midst of life's most difficult struggles. Before the worship service begins, prepare a 5½X8½-inch sheet of paper to be inserted into each bulletin or handed out by the ushers at the appropriate time. As you prepare the sheet, type "Menu" at the top in bold letters, and then make enough copies for everyone in attendance.

Say: **Psalm 23 teaches us to express our satisfaction in the care of the Great Shepherd. It reminds us that no matter how difficult our journey, we are assured of the comfort of God's love and goodness. For even in the presence of our enemies, God prepares a table for us. Unfortunately, the greatest abundance is nothing more than a dry pasture to those who do not hear the voice of the Shepherd. But those who hear his voice through faith discover green pastures all around.**

As you introduce the idea that life's valleys can be fruitful since God's feast is always before us, challenge your listeners to think of the items God might spread on the table he has prepared.

At the appropriate point in your sermon, have the listeners write on their menus the spiritual items they believe God would serve at his table. After everyone has had an opportunity to note a few items, ask participants to form small discussion groups of four or five people each.

As they assemble in their groups, ask them to share their menu items with one another. After approximately five minutes, ask: **If you could choose just one item from your menu that has best represented God's love and goodness during a difficult time in your life, what would it be?**

After allowing your listeners a moment to ponder, ask them to share their thoughts with the others in their groups. After approximately five minutes, ask for a few volunteers to share with the congregation the most important menu items God has placed before them on his table.

Continue your sermon, describing the ways in which God provides lavish hospitality and abundant protection all the days of our lives.

Reprinted from *Off the Church Wall* by Rob Portlock. © 1987 by Rob Portlock.
Used by permission of InterVarsity Press, P.O. Box 1400, Downers Grove, IL 60515.

The Workers Are Few

TOPIC: MAKING A DIFFERENCE IN THE LIVES OF OTHERS

SCRIPTURE: MATTHEW 9:35-38

This short, narrated drama will help your listeners better understand their roles in responding to Jesus' call for workers to go into the harvest field and bring souls to Christ.

Prior to the worship service, ask one male teenager and one older male adult to help you present a short drama. There are no speaking parts; you will provide all the narration. Practicing the drama two or three times before the actual event will cause it to run more smoothly and make it more effective.

Identify ahead of time an appropriate cue on which the actors will enter. Begin the drama by having the teenager walk to the front of the congregation. After a moment's pause, he should begin wandering around, acting as if he is reaching down, picking up objects, and gently tossing them out into the ocean.

Begin your narration as the two act out the drama:

One day, a very old man was walking down the beach and noticed a young boy picking up starfish and throwing them into the sea. When he caught up with the boy, he asked the boy what he was doing. The boy answered that because of the morning tide, many starfish were stranded and would die if they were exposed to the hot sun any longer.

In amazement the man said, "This beach goes on for miles. There are millions of starfish that will die. How can what you do make any real difference?"

The young boy picked up another starfish, looked at it, and said, "It makes a difference to this one." Then he threw it into the safety of the ocean. (At this point the two actors walk off together.)

Ask the listeners to join one or two other people and discuss the following two questions with them:

● **How did this drama relate to Jesus' statement that "the harvest is plentiful but the workers are few"?**

VIEW FROM THE PEW

There are many folks who will respond to a creative presentation of the gospel who would really never respond to a regular sermon.

● In response to Jesus' request for workers to go into the harvest field, what are some of the little things we can do that might make a difference in others' lives?

Continue your sermon, discussing the commission Jesus has given us as laborers in his field.

PASTOR WAGMAN KNEW HE WAS ON A ROLL WHEN THE CONGREGATION STARTED DOING THE WAVE.

Reprinted from *McPherson Goes to Church* by John McPherson. © 1994 John McPherson. Used by permission.

For the Sake of Others

HIGH
MEDIUM
LOW

RISK RATING

TOPIC: SPIRITUAL GIFTS

SCRIPTURE: 1 CORINTHIANS 12:3-13

This activity will help listeners better understand that the Holy Spirit gives us gifts not so much for our own sake but for the sake of others. We have received spiritual gifts so we can bless others by ministering to them. Paul makes this clear when he writes, "To each one the manifestation of the Spirit is given for the common good" (1 Corinthians 12:7).

Before the worship service, slice enough apples so that everyone in your congregation can have a slice. (**Note:** Either spray lemon juice on the slices or soak them in Sprite to keep them from turning brown. Be sure to cover and refrigerate them until just before the sermon.) Next, make a list of spiritual gifts. (Most of them can be found in Romans 12:6-8; 1 Corinthians 12:8-10; Ephesians 4:11-12; and 1 Peter 4:10-11.) Use a marker to write each gift on the top of a separate piece of poster board or newsprint. Before the worship service, tape the sheets to the walls of the room you will be using. Include an additional sheet with nothing written on it. If the listeners do not have access to a pen or pencil, provide one near each sheet.

At the beginning of your sermon or at another appropriate point, have the ushers distribute plates of apple slices. Invite the congregation to enjoy eating the fruit. After everyone has been served, pose this riddle:

● **What holds an apple but never eats it?** (Hopefully, someone will provide the correct answer: an apple tree. If no one provides the answer, you'll need to answer the question yourself.) Reinforce the answer to this riddle by saying: **We are like apple trees in that we produce fruit, not for ourselves, but for others. Your gifts are given to you for the purpose of blessing others as you minister to them. If you have the gift of teaching, you have it so others in the body will be taught. If you've been given the gift of compassion, it is so you will be understanding and sympathetic toward others. If you cannot readily identify a gift in your life, be** assured that God has given you one. It often takes time to discover our gifts.

Next, have all the participants stand and move to the sheet that best describes their predominant spiritual gift. Tell those who are unable to locate their spiritual gifts to assemble at the blank sheet.

Once participants are standing by the sheets that best describe their spiritual gifts, have them each write their names on the sheet and then spend a moment telling others in their group one way in which they have used that gift. Have those assembled at the blank page write both their names and their spiritual gifts. (**Note:** Parents or other adults may need to direct children if they are present.) Depending on your group size, allow between five and ten minutes for this portion of the activity.

You may want to leave the sheets taped to the wall for two or three weeks to remind everyone of the wealth of spiritual gifts in the congregation. Or you may want to collect the sheets and print their contents in an upcoming church newsletter or bulletin.

"That was the best sermon on giving I've ever heard."

Open the Door

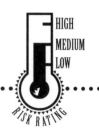

RISK RATING

TOPIC: GRACE

SCRIPTURE: TITUS 2:11-14

This activity will remind those present that while grace and salvation are available to all people, they can be either accepted or rejected.

As an effective beginning to your sermon, enter your meeting place wearing a fishing hat or other fishing garb and carrying a fishing pole over your shoulder. Sit in a chair where everyone can see you, and flip your fishing line away from you a few feet. Sit as though you were fishing and becoming frustrated because you were catching nothing. After a minute or so, ask for a show of hands from all those who have ever gone fishing and caught nothing.

Say: **With such good bait on the line, it's hard to understand why so many fish choose not to take it. Why do you suppose that is?** Wait for someone to respond.

Say: **In our Scripture lesson today, we are reminded that God's saving grace is available to everyone, but the fact is, not everyone accepts it.**

Have everyone in your congregation pair up with someone else. Instruct each pair to read Titus 2:11-14. Next, ask pairs to discuss the following question:

If grace is offered as a free gift to everyone, why do some choose not to accept it?

After three or four minutes of discussion, describe the well-known painting by the artist Holman Hunt of Jesus standing and knocking at a door. **(Note:** This activity will be even more effective if you have a print of the painting to share with your congregation.) As you are describing the painting, remind the congregation that the odd part of the picture is that there is no doorknob on the outside of the door on which Jesus is knocking.

Ask the pair partners to discuss why the artist may have chosen to exclude the outside doorknob from the painting. (Most of the discussion will probably focus on our obligation to answer the door from the inside.) Allow two or three minutes for discussion, and then

VIEW FROM THE PEW

What I like least about sermons is...long, drawn-out explanations with no attention getters.

ask a few people to share their thoughts with everyone.

Continue your sermon, focusing on the fact that God's saving grace is universally available.

PASTOR DAVE CALHOON WAS TRYING DESPERATELY TO MAKE HIS SERMONS MORE LIVELY.

Reprinted from *McPherson Goes to Church* by John McPherson. © 1994 John McPherson. Used by permission.

Where Was Jesus?

HIGH
MEDIUM
LOW

RISK RATING

TOPIC: GOD'S LOVE
SCRIPTURE: JOHN 11:1-45

This activity will encourage participants to turn their painful memories and feelings over to God.

Before the service, place a cardboard box on the altar or in another prominent spot. Cut a slot in the top of the box so pieces of paper can be slid through it. Distribute pieces of paper and pencils to members of the congregation as they arrive and are seated.

Read the Bible passage aloud, then say: **Mary and Martha agreed on at least one thing: If Jesus had been there earlier, Lazarus wouldn't have died. Jesus' journey shouldn't have taken more than a few hours, but he showed up several days after he was sent for. Where was Jesus when Lazarus needed him?**

Write down an instance in your life when you've asked the question "Where was Jesus?" Maybe it was when a child died suddenly or a parent died slowly of a painful disease. Maybe your memory is of a failed marriage or a corporate downsizing that sent your family into financial distress. It's OK to have the painful feelings associated with these memories, but God wants us to turn them over to him. In a moment we will have an opportunity to symbolically give our painful memories to God.

Assure people that no one will see what they write. The object is for them to slip their pieces of paper into the box, which will be destroyed later.

Allow participants one minute to write their memories; then ask one section of your congregation at a time to come forward and drop the papers into the box. (Avoid the temptation to open the box. Personally destroy it without glancing at its contents.)

When this activity is complete, read John 11:14 and continue to speak about the losses that even faithful Christians may experience.

HIGH
MEDIUM
LOW

RISK RATING

Instant Theater

TOPIC: JESUS' AUTHORITY AND POWER
SCRIPTURE: MARK 4:35-41

Use this short skit to illustrate Jesus' power and authority.

Recruit four volunteers, and assign each of them one of the following parts: James, John, Jesus, and the Weather. Position them and the following props so that the audience can easily see them. Place two folding chairs side-by-side to create a boat bench on which James and John will sit. Place another chair in the back (stern) of your "boat," and have Jesus sit there. Give a spray bottle (set to deliver a fine mist) filled with clean water to the Weather.

After introducing the Scripture passage, ask the characters to pantomime their parts as you read the following paraphrase of Mark 4:35-41: **When evening came, Jesus said to his disciples, "Let us go over to the other side of the lake." Leaving the crowd behind, they took him along, just as he was, in the boat.**

A light breeze was blowing. (Pause.) **As James and John rowed slowly** (pause), **all the disciples watched the sunset. They didn't notice that large clouds were billowing behind them.** (Pause.)

Soon the boat began to rock as large waves hit it. (Pause.) **Spray flew over the bow of the ship.** (Pause.) **James and John rowed furiously.** (Pause.)

Jesus was in the stern of the boat, sleeping on a cushion. (Pause.) **The disciples woke him and said to him, "Teacher, don't you care if we drown?"** (Pause.)

Jesus rose to his feet and rebuked the wind. (Pause.) **He said to the waves, "Quiet! Be still!"** (Pause.) **Then the wind died down, and it was completely calm.** (Pause.)

Jesus said to his disciples, "Why are you so afraid? Do you still have no faith?" (Pause.)

The disciples were terrified and asked each other, "Who is this? Even the wind and the waves obey him!"

VIEW FROM THE PEW

The best sermons are... ones that are presented differently and in a way that encourages us to search the Scriptures.

Cookies

HIGH
MEDIUM
LOW

RISK RATING

TOPIC: SPIRITUAL MATURITY
SCRIPTURE: 1 CORINTHIANS 3:1-9

Use this activity to introduce the idea of spiritual maturity in a particularly tasty way! As members of your congregation arrive, distribute a small cookie to everyone at the door. Tell everyone *not* to eat the cookie—yet.

Begin the activity by holding up a baby-food jar of strained spinach. Open the lid. Describe the smell and consistency.

Next, hold up a cookie. Point out that it's mouthwatering, full of sweet flavor, perhaps packed with chocolate chips. Describe the inviting taste of the cookie in detail; then ask the participants to enjoy their snack together.

As people eat their cookies, read 1 Corinthians 3:1-9. Say: **Paul labeled these Christians in Corinth infants in the Christian life because they weren't yet spiritually mature. They weren't yet ready for mature food, just as a small baby wouldn't be ready to eat a cookie. The Corinthians didn't yet have control of their desires. God's desire for us is to move beyond spiritual infancy into a mature Christian life. Just as you can't live on baby food your entire life, it takes substantial food to grow, and that's true spiritually, too.**

VIEW FROM THE PEW

Would you like to see your pastor try some new methods other than lecture during the sermon time?... Yes! Something to get everyone involved.

Come With Me

TOPIC: FOLLOWING JESUS

SCRIPTURE: MATTHEW 4:13-20

This passage is so familiar that often it loses its power. Here's one way to involve your audience in a bit of the tension that certainly accompanied the events described in the passage.

During your sermon, at a prearranged point, have a conspirator walk into the back of the sanctuary and say loudly, "Pastor, come with me. Now!"

Respond with shock (unless being called away from your pulpit in midsermon is a common occurrence!), but quickly regain your composure. Gather up your sermon notes, and quickly walk through the sanctuary and out the door. Don't stop until you're out of sight.

Let thirty seconds pass before you return. It will be the longest thirty seconds ever experienced in your church—guaranteed!

When you return, continue your sermon from the back of the sanctuary and trace your steps back toward the pulpit. Pause while you're still standing in the aisle between rows of people and say: **What you saw is like what Peter's and Andrew's friends saw. Perhaps you even had some of the same thoughts that their friends had.**

Ask for volunteers to share what they thought was happening when you were called away. Don't return to the pulpit until you've received input from your audience.

Raise the risk rating of this experience by having the participants turn to partners and discuss the following questions:

● **Has following Jesus ever required you to walk away from something or someone you valued? Explain.**

● **On a scale of one to ten, how well do you follow where Jesus leads?**

Three and Out

HIGH
MEDIUM
LOW

RISK RATING

TOPIC: RESPONDING TO GOD
SCRIPTURE: 1 SAMUEL 3:1-10

Use this idea during your sermon to highlight the idea that God's voice is sometimes difficult to recognize—and often interrupts people's plans and schedules.

You'll need two cell phones and a reliable conspirator who is positioned where he or she can see you but is out of sight of the congregation. Place one cell phone in your pocket, and give the other to your helper.

Arrange a time during your sermon for your friend to call you, prompting you to pull out your cell phone, apologize, and take the call.

Be abrupt on the phone. Listen for two seconds and dismiss the caller by saying: **Look, I don't care what you're selling! I don't need it! Goodbye!**

Pocket the phone, apologize again, and resume your sermon. After a sentence or two, have your friend call you again. Repeat the procedure, but be even more forceful by speaking immediately without listening. Say: **I told you before. This is a terrible time to talk, and I'm not interested!**

When the phone rings a third time, communicate both that you're quite embarrassed and furious. When you answer the phone, act as though you are very angry and almost unable to speak. Let your face soften as you realize it's your mother calling (or father or brother—someone who might call from a long distance). Say, **Oh, hi, Mom. Was that you who called earlier? Twice?** (Pause.) **Are you remembering what time it is here?** (Pause.) **That's right. Actually, I'm preaching...right now. OK, call you back later.**

Put the phone back in your pocket. Say: **What just happened was done to illustrate a point. How many people miss important messages from God because they're busy with other tasks? Too often, we either consider God's voice an interruption, or we never hear it because we're not listening.**

Raise the risk rating of this experience by asking your audience to form small groups and discuss the following questions:

● How was this experience like or unlike what happened in the Scripture passage?

● On a scale of one to ten, how well do you listen to God?

● In what ways have you heard messages from God? Share some of your stories.

PASTOR LIMKIN WAS EXTREMELY DISAPPOINTED WHEN HE DISCOVERED THAT THE CONGREGATION'S SHOW OF TOGETHERNESS WAS ACTUALLY CAUSED BY A BROKEN FURNACE.

Reprinted from *McPherson Goes to Church* by John McPherson. © 1994 John McPherson. Used by permission.

Crisp Clap

RISK RATING

TOPIC: UNITY

SCRIPTURE: ROMANS 15:4-13

This illustration will help you experience both the visual and the auditory elements of unity. Romans 15:5 is a powerful challenge for the church. We often talk about unity but rarely get a glimpse of how it looks or sounds.

After announcing your subject, tell the congregation that you are going to attempt something that involves them. Ask the participants to put down whatever they have in their hands and pay close attention. Lift your hands above your head with your palms facing each other. Then count: **One, two, clap.** On the word "clap," bring your hands together to make a clapping sound.

To involve your congregation members, ask them to stand. Say: **Let's all do this activity together after I give the count. Are you ready? One, two, clap!** Hopefully, you will hear a solid, unified clap. You may need to repeat the exercise until it is completely unified. It is amazing how singular this clap will be as each person pays close attention to your instructions. Have the participants give their neighbors a high five before being seated.

Continue your sermon, discussing how simple the steps really are to accomplish a very simple act of unity.

VIEW FROM THE PEW

One encouraging thought I'd like to share with people who deliver sermons is...Be willing to risk and change.

Tongue Trouble

TOPIC: CONTROLLING THE TONGUE

SCRIPTURE: JAMES 3:1-12

VIEW FROM THE PEW

I like sermons that...creatively bring out a point that helps me in my daily walk.

This activity works well to illustrate the need to control the words that come out of our mouths.

When you are ready to begin, say: **Christians often forget that controlling the tongue must be done internally through the renewing of the mind and spirit. No matter how hard people try to repair their language habits, change occurs only with complete surrender to God. My plan is to demonstrate this point by asking you, in a moment, to repeat a tongue twister. The phrase is "Tiny Toby's tongue told Timmy Toddle terribly troublesome truths today."**

(**Note:** You may want to write the phrase ahead of time on a piece of newsprint and post it where the participants can see it. Or you may want to display it with an overhead projector.)

Lead participants in saying the tongue twister together, and then ask them to repeat it quickly three times in a row. Afterward, say: **This simple illustration reveals that it is difficult to control our tongues through our own strength. We often try to manufacture change through manipulation, control, or physical power. The truth is that what comes from our tongues will change only as we submit ourselves to God's control.**

Have the participants pair up with someone else and respond to the following discussion questions:

● When do you have the most trouble controlling your tongue?

● What are some ways you try to change these habits by your own strength?

● How can you offer control of your tongue to God?

The Band-Aid Doctor

HIGH
MEDIUM
LOW

RISK RATING

TOPIC: HEALING THE WOUNDED

SCRIPTURE: LUKE 10:30-37

The story of the good Samaritan is a great example of how we're to treat people who are hurting. Before the worship service, place Band-Aids in containers. Be sure there are enough Band-Aids for everyone in the congregation.

After speaking on this text, instruct the ushers to come forward and hand out Band-Aids to members of the congregation. After all the participants have received a Band-Aid, have them each peel off the backing and place the Band-Aid on the finger of the person next to them. When the activity is complete, everyone should have a Band-Aid on his or her finger. Challenge the participants to commit to wearing their Band-Aids for a couple of days.

Say: **The Band-Aid on your finger will be a reminder to watch for wounded and hurting people as you go through your day. Remember that a kind word, a thoughtful act, or a meaningful smile can be a Band-Aid to someone who is hurting.**

The Power of a Promise

TOPIC: PROMISES

SCRIPTURE: GENESIS 9:8-17

VIEW FROM THE PEW

What I like least about sermons is...when I'm not quite sure what point the pastor is trying to make.

Use this idea to illustrate the fact that love motivates us to make promises.

After reading the story of God's promise to Noah, pause and say: **God's promises are motivated by his powerful love for us. Let's see if we can come closer to understanding just how powerful that love is.**

Form groups of three or four. Have all the people in each group either remove their wedding rings or other symbols—such as cross necklaces or friendship bracelets—of some type of love relationship. When everyone is ready, have all those holding a symbolic item explain

- what the symbol they're holding represents to them,
- what the item symbolizes to other people who see it, and
- why the symbol is important.

After the discussion, have everyone hold up the items so that everyone else can see them. Then say: **Look around at all the symbols we carry to express our commitment to the special people in our lives. These symbols are important because they remind us of who we are and what's important to us. In the same way, the rainbow is God's symbol of his promise to us. It's not just a symbol about flooding the earth. It's a symbol of his love.**

After participants have put their items back on, continue your sermon.

Drowning Out God

HIGH
MEDIUM
LOW

RISK RATING

TOPIC: COMPLAINING

SCRIPTURE: EXODUS 17:1-7

Use this idea to help people understand that an attitude of constant complaining can drown out God's presence in their lives.

After reading about the Israelites' complaints to Moses, illustrate the point by dividing the audience into six sections. Give participants in each group the following instructions:

● **Group 1—Think of three things men complain about.**

● **Group 2—Think of three things women complain about.**

● **Group 3—Think of three things teenagers and children complain about.**

● **Group 4—Think of three things parents complain about.**

● **Group 5—Think of three things employees complain about.**

● **Group 6—Think of three things Christians complain about.**

Have the members of group 1 stand and begin repeating out loud the three things they chose. Once group 1 is speaking, add group 2, then group 3, and so on. When all the groups are speaking at once, have a soloist with a microphone start singing "Immanuel" or another song about God's presence and love in our lives. As the soloist sings, quiet each group in turn so that the music eventually becomes clear.

After the song, have congregation members turn to a partner and discuss the following questions:

● **Were you able to hear the music well over the grumbling? Why or why not?**

● **How does a complaining attitude drown out God's presence in our lives?**

● **What can we do to avoid this problem?**

When pairs have finished their discussions, continue your sermon.

Obedience in Small Ways

TOPIC: OBEDIENCE

SCRIPTURE: 2 KINGS 5:1-14

Use this activity to demonstrate the value of obeying God even when the task seems trivial or beneath us.

Before the sermon, make enough copies of the "Award Certificate" handout (p. 69) so that each participant can have one. Complete three of the awards for three individuals in your church who volunteer their time to do thankless jobs around the church or community—a nursery worker (the Diaper-Changing Dynamo), the janitor (the Terrific Tile Cleaner), or the church treasurer (the Money Master), for example. To add to the experience, you might want to include a small gift, such as a gift certificate to a local restaurant or popular store.

What makes a sermon memorable for you?...One that makes a clear point.

Sometime during the sermon, say: **At first, Naaman didn't want to obey God because he felt God's command was too menial for someone in his position. He didn't understand that true success comes not from grand acts of sacrifice and love in the name of God. Success comes through a willingness to obey God in the little things, even when those things seem trivial or thankless.**

Call the three award winners forward, and describe the ways they each contribute to others in their "small" ways. Then present the awards.

Say: **We have each felt the benefit of someone else's small acts of kindness or thankless generosity. Today is a good time to recognize those people in our lives.**

Have the ushers distribute a blank certificate to each person in the audience. Next, ask the participants to each think of one person in their lives who obeys God by serving others in small ways, someone who does so without expecting anything in return. Have the participants complete their certificates for those persons. Encourage participants to present the certificates after the worship service.

Once the certificates have been distributed, close the activity with a round of applause for all those who obey God in the "small ways." Then continue your sermon.

Award Certificate

On this _____ day of _____

I hereby declare that I am eternally grateful to this special person in my life:

_____

I want you to know that your consistent obedience to God in the "small" things has made a "big" difference in my life. To be specific:

_____

I offer you this certificate to say thank you for your selfless love and concern for others.

Signed,

_____

A Terrible Intimacy

TOPIC: BEING KNOWN BY GOD

SCRIPTURE: PSALM 139:1-12

This activity will help participants better understand what it can feel like to be intimately known by God. Begin by having congregation members pair off. On your command, have the partners make and maintain direct eye contact with each other for sixty seconds. After the experience, have each pair join another pair to discuss the following questions:

● **What was your reaction to this experience?**

● **Why is it so hard to look into someone's eyes for an extended time?**

● **How is this experience like or unlike your reaction to God's searching gaze into your heart?**

● **How is your feeling in this experience like the feeling of knowing God intimately? of God knowing you intimately?**

After allowing for an appropriate period for discussion, continue your sermon.

Gifts for the King

HIGH
MEDIUM
LOW

RISK RATING

TOPIC: WORSHIP (CHRISTMAS)

SCRIPTURE: MATTHEW 2:1-12

This activity can be used to enrich a Christmas worship experience or sermon.

Before the service, set up a makeshift manger in the front of the room. You might consider using a wooden crate or trough and filling it with hay.

As you guide your congregation through the Scripture passage, note that those who came to see Jesus were compelled to worship him (not a typical response among most adults when they see babies). Say: **Like the people in this passage, we want to worship Jesus too—especially now, at Christmastime.**

Have ushers distribute index cards to the audience members. Ask them each to write one reason they want to worship Jesus this Christmas. After everyone has finished, have participants rise and move single file past the manger. As each person reaches the manger, have him or her kneel for a moment and place the card in the manger. (If your church is too large to do this, simply have the audience kneel in place while the ushers collect the index cards and place them in the manger.) While congregation members move past the manger, have your song leader lead the congregation in singing worshipful Christmas music.

HIGH
MEDIUM
LOW

RISK RATING

Guided Tours

TOPIC: FAITH

SCRIPTURE: MATTHEW 14:22-33

Use this idea to help your congregation experience what it's like to have faith as Peter did.

At some point during your sermon, say: **I want you to experience what it must have been like for Peter to trust Jesus. Everyone, choose a partner. Within your pair, take turns closing your eyes and letting your partner guide you around the room. Your partner may use only his or her voice to guide you—no touching allowed. Make sure both partners get a turn.**

After everyone has both guided and been guided, ask participants to discuss the following questions with their partners:

● **What was your reaction to this experience?**

● **How was focusing on your partner's voice like the way Peter focused on Jesus during the storm?**

● **What made Peter lose faith?**

● **What makes you lose faith?**

● **How can we develop stronger faith?**

After the discussion, continue your sermon.

Like a Thief

HIGH
MEDIUM
LOW

RISK RATING

TOPIC: THE SECOND COMING
SCRIPTURE: MATTHEW 24:36-44

Use this idea to demonstrate in a memorable way the nature of Christ's return.

A few days before the service, ask a volunteer to assist you with this activity by hiding just outside or near the platform area with a pair of cymbals (or another loud instrument such as a trumpet).

As your sermon progresses, read the passage aloud; then ask each person to quietly read it again. Midway through the reading, silently signal the volunteer to step inside the room and quickly crash the cymbals (or blast the trumpet). (**Note:** If your church building is large, you might want to heighten the effect by having the volunteer step up to a nearby microphone.)

After the shock wears off, have folks turn to a partner and discuss these questions:

● **How was this experience like the way Christ will come again?**

● **Were you expecting the crash** [or blast]**? Why or why not?**

● **What can we do to "keep watch" so that we'll be ready when Christ returns?**

After the discussion, continue your sermon.

A Picture of Repentance

TOPIC: REPENTANCE

SCRIPTURE: MARK 1:4-11

Use this creative experience to guide people through the act of repentance.

Toward the end of the sermon, say: **John preached a message of repentance from sins, a message that God continues to speak today. Let's take a few moments to creatively reflect on the need all of us have for repentance.**

Have the congregation stand, and instruct the organist or musicians to play quietly in the background. Then guide the participants through the following instructions:

If you've ever done or said something that wrongfully injured another person, fold your arms.

If you've ever been judgmental, or if you've ever let your eyes look at things of which God does not approve, close your eyes.

If you've ever made a conscious choice to disobey God and do what you wanted rather than what God wanted, turn halfway around.

Sin closes us off from the presence of God and also from relationship with others. Sin leads to isolation and eventually to death. But God has provided a way out through repentance and forgiveness.

If you've ever asked God to forgive you for not following his will in your life, lower your arms.

If you've ever made a conscious decision not to judge others, even when rumors abounded, open your eyes.

If you've ever turned away from a sinful habit and turned to God for strength and guidance, turn back around and face the front.

If you are willing to repent humbly and quickly whenever you sin against God and others, I'd like you to kneel where you are.

Once everyone is kneeling, pray: **Lord, right now we kneel before you in humble repentance for the sins we commit against you and others. As we spend a moment in silence, I ask you to**

VIEW FROM THE PEW

What I like least about sermons is...a dry delivery.

bring to mind in each of us any sin for which we need to ask forgiveness. Thank you for your willingness to wipe the slate clean in each of our hearts. Let's pray silently.

After a minute of silence, close the experience by saying: **In Jesus' name, amen.**

HIGH
MEDIUM
LOW

RISK RATING

Defining Success

TOPIC: SUCCESS

SCRIPTURE: MARK 12:28-34

Use this idea to challenge people to redefine success in their lives according to Christ's teachings.

At the beginning of the service, before you read the Scripture passage, say: **Today we're going to talk about the secret of true success in life. To begin, I'd like to find out your definition of real success. So we're going to take a quick survey.**

Have ushers distribute index cards; then say: **On your card, write down and complete this statement, "A truly successful person is one who..."** When everyone has finished, collect the cards, and have a few volunteers tally the results. Say: **We'll announce the results of the survey at the end of the sermon.**

Begin your sermon, focusing on the Scripture passage as the answer to the survey statement. Near the end of your sermon, say: **Now that we know how Jesus would complete our survey statement, let's see how close we came to his response.**

Announce the survey results, and note how the congregation's response was similar to or different from Jesus' message. Then say: **Let me close the message by leading you in a responsive prayer. Close your eyes and repeat after me.**

O Lord our God, you are the one true God.
Help us to love you with all our heart,
Guide us to love you with all our soul,
Inspire us to love you with all our mind,
Challenge us to love you with all our strength, and
Encourage us to love our neighbors
As much as we love ourselves.
These are the greatest commandments, Lord.
This is what true success means.
Help us to see it,
To know it,
To live it. In Jesus' name, amen.

VIEW FROM THE PEW

Would you like to see your pastor try some new methods other than lecture during the sermon time?... Yes! People have different learning styles. If you're trying to teach, you should use a variety.

Savior in Disguise

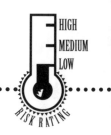

HIGH
MEDIUM
LOW

RISK RATING

TOPIC: RECOGNIZING JESUS
SCRIPTURE: JOHN 1:10-18

Use this idea to illustrate the idea that the world did not recognize Jesus when he came.

About a week or so before the service, ask some volunteers to secretly help you prepare for this experience by collecting dirty, old clothes for you to wear. If possible, ask a local makeup artist to disguise your face to look like a weathered, homeless person. Find a hat to complete the disguise.

On the day of the service, put on your disguise and come into the church just a few minutes before the service is scheduled to begin. Walk slowly to the front and take a seat in the second or third row. If anyone talks to you, respond kindly, but act shy.

When it's time to begin, have another leader in the church stand before the congregation and say: **Due to an unforeseen circumstance, our pastor is unable to be with us today. However, a guest speaker has agreed to speak in our pastor's place.**

With that introduction, stand up and move to the front of the room. Without introducing yourself, begin the sermon simply by reading aloud John 1:10-18. After the reading, ask the congregation:

● **How many of you know who I am?**

If necessary, help people recognize you by removing your hat or another part of your disguise. Have participants form groups of three or four to discuss these questions:

● **What did you think when you first saw me this morning?**

● **How is that like the way many people responded to Jesus when he came?**

● **What did it take for you to recognize me?**

● **What did it take for people to recognize Jesus when he came?**

● **What would it take for you to recognize Jesus now?**

For your convenience, you may want to write the questions on an overhead transparency. Use the group discussion period to leave and change your clothes. Then, after you return and the discussions are over, continue your sermon.

Abide in the Vine

TOPIC: SUBMISSION TO CHRIST

SCRIPTURE: JOHN 15:1-8

Use this idea to illustrate the difference between people who submit to Christ and those who don't.

A few days before the service, collect enough dead twigs and small branches for each person in the congregation to have one. Also collect enough pieces of fruit to hand out to everyone.

Toward the end of your sermon, say: **Let me use an illustration to help explain the vast difference that exists between those who submit to Christ and those who don't.**

Have the ushers distribute the dead twigs and branches to the congregation members. Instruct the participants to form groups of four to work together to find any signs of life in the twigs they have received. After a minute or so, get everyone's attention, and ask the whole congregation:

- **Can these twigs grow? Why not?**
- **Can these twigs produce fruit? Why not?**
- **Are they good for anything, except to be thrown into the fire? Why not?**

Say: **This is what people are like spiritually when they fail to remain in Christ. Now let's contrast that with those who submit to Christ.**

Have the ushers distribute a piece of fruit to each person in the congregation. Have participants return to their foursomes and, as before, look for signs of life. Then get everyone's attention and ask:

- **What makes this fruit attractive?**
- **What's this fruit good for?**
- **This is what people are like spiritually when they submit to Christ. What is the difference?**

If you desire, have the congregation members eat the fruit together as an act of thanksgiving for God's abundant grace.

Our Weakness in Prayer

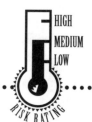

HIGH
MEDIUM
LOW

RISK RATING

TOPIC: PRAYER

SCRIPTURE: ROMANS 8:22-27

Use this experience to demonstrate why we need the Spirit to intercede for us.

Toward the end of your sermon, say: **Let's see if we can experience what this passage is talking about. Let's seek God in prayer silently for the next five minutes. Pray for whatever God lays on your heart.**

After five minutes of silence, close the prayer time and ask:

● **How many of you were distracted at times during our silent prayer?**

● **How many of you weren't sure what to pray about?**

After a show of hands, say: **Some of us just experienced our weakness before God. We couldn't even pray effectively for five minutes. Others may have had a great time of prayer. Either way, it's great to know that the Spirit is constantly interceding for us.**

VIEW FROM THE PEW

What I like least about sermons is...communicating God's word only through lecture.

HIGH
MEDIUM
LOW

RISK RATING

Self-Righteousness

TOPIC: FAITH AND DEEDS

SCRIPTURE: JAMES 2:14-17

VIEW FROM THE PEW

One encouraging thought I'd like to share with people who deliver sermons is...The more creative you are, the more the Word speaks to the congregation's heart.

Use this skit as a discussion starter during a sermon on the difference between Christian faith and deeds.

Recruit three people to perform the skit. Give each one a photocopy of the "Love vs. Knowledge" script (pp. 81-82), and arrange for the trio to rehearse at least once before the service.

After the skit, have congregation members form pairs to discuss the following questions:

● Which character in the skit did you identify with most? Why?

● What lessons can be learned from this skit about the value of love over knowledge?

After the discussion, continue your sermon.

LOVE VS. KNOWLEDGE

THE SCENE

This skit takes place outside a church building on a Sunday morning. The church service has just ended, and people are returning to their cars.

THE CHARACTERS

Kathy: A young, pregnant lady who has just been seriously injured in a hit-and-run car accident. She is dressed simply and has dirt on her clothes, head, and hands.

Brent: A loving Christian man. He is dressed for church and carrying a Bible.

Susan: A knowledgeable Christian woman. She is dressed for church and carrying a Bible.

THE SKIT

(As the scene opens, Brent and Susan are walking onstage, making small talk about the day's sermon. As they talk, Kathy crawls onstage from the opposite side.)

Kathy: Excuse me, I need help…Please!

(Brent runs to help her. Susan stands still and folds her arms around her Bible.)

Brent: *(Helping her up)* Are you all right? What happened?

Susan: Brent, you shouldn't touch her like that. You don't know where she's been.

Brent: Nonsense, Susan. She's just hurt. *(To Kathy)* Come on. *(They walk to where Susan is standing.)*

Susan: So what happened to you, dear?

Kathy: I was hit by a car.

Susan: Oh, really? Where were you?

Kathy: I don't remember. I think on Fifty-third Street.

Susan: Well…that's a very dangerous street. I would certainly never even go near the traffic there. It's a stupid thing to do.

Brent: Susan, please. Can't you see she's injured?

Susan: Well, I'm only saying what's true. She wouldn't be hurt if she'd just stayed away from dangerous places like that. It's her own fault. And I think she knows that.

Kathy: I'm sorry. I shouldn't have come here. *(Looks at Brent.)* If you could just help me down these stairs…

Brent: Nonsense! You're coming inside, and we're going to call an ambulance. We'll take care of you; don't worry.

Susan: *(To Kathy)* Um, just one moment, dear. *(Motions for Brent to come aside, then whispers to him.)* I don't think you should take her inside the church, Brent.

Brent: *(Aggravated)* Why not?

Susan: Well, look at her! *(Gestures at Kathy.)* She's a mess!

Brent: *(Angry)* Susan, I don't know what your problem is, but right now, I don't care. This girl needs our help, and I, for one, am going to give it to her. I think your attitude is pathetic.

Susan: Is that so? Well, I guess I'll just have to spell it out for you. *(To Kathy)* Young lady, did the car hit you this morning?

Kathy: Yes, just about half an hour ago.

Susan: So you weren't in church this morning?

Kathy: No. I don't go to church much.

Susan: *(Looking at Brent)* There, you see? She got what she deserved. If she had been in church instead of roaming the streets, this would never have happened. You won't be helping her by tending to her wounds. She needs to realize that she chose this for herself. She needs to feel the pain of her choices. It's wrong to help her, Brent. And I won't be a part of it.

Brent: *(Looking sad, shaking his head)* Susan, you just don't get it, do you?

A Sacrifice of Giving

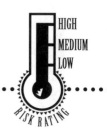

HIGH
MEDIUM
LOW

RISK RATING

TOPIC: OUTREACH

SCRIPTURE: 2 CORINTHIANS 9:6-15

Use this powerful experience to challenge congregation members to sow in faith.

(Note: You'll want to get the approval of your church's leadership before using this idea.)

During the week prior to the service, have church leaders gather and make a list of all the people in your congregation who have special financial needs. Some examples might include single moms, the unemployed, those facing special medical crises, and so forth.

On the day of the service, take the offering early. While you continue with the service, have church leaders count the offering in private and divide it equally among all those on the list you created. Have the treasurer write out checks to each of the recipients and place each check in a separate envelope with the appropriate person's name written on it.

At the end of the sermon, say: **I'm going to ask you to join with me in a daring act of faith to demonstrate our belief in the value of sowing generously, as the Scripture teaches.**

Show the stack of envelopes to the congregation and say: **This is today's offering. There are several individuals and families within our congregation who have special financial needs. As an act of faith, we are going to offer this money to them as we practice giving sacrificially. The envelopes will be mailed out from the church office this week.**

Offer a special prayer of thanksgiving for the offering and a special blessing for those who will receive the gifts.

(Note: If you feel your congregation is not yet ready to give away the entire offering in this manner, offer only a portion of it instead. Also, you might vary the gifts according to the individual recipients' needs.)

VIEW FROM THE PEW

The one suggestion for improvement that I'd share with people who deliver sermons is...Involve the congregation.

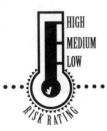

HIGH
MEDIUM
LOW

RISK RATING

Blessing One Another

TOPIC: INTERCESSION

SCRIPTURE: EPHESIANS 1:15-23

Use this prayer activity in guiding people to use Paul's words to encourage one another.

As a creative way to end your sermon, have people form pairs and stand facing each other. Say: **In closing, let's take a moment to paraphrase Paul's words in Ephesians as a blessing for each other.** Have the partner who's wearing the most red begin.

Say: **Look into your partner's eyes and repeat this blessing, phrase by phrase, after me:**

I pray to the God of our Lord Jesus Christ
That he would give you the Spirit of wisdom and revelation
So that you may know him better.

Then have the other person look at his or her partner and repeat the following phrases after you:

I pray that the eyes of your heart may be enlightened
So that you may know the hope to which he has called you
And the riches of his glorious inheritance
And his great power given to us who believe.

Then have the entire congregation complete the blessing by repeating these words after you:

May we all know this power,
A power that raised Christ from the dead
And seated him at the right hand of God in heaven.
Christ is far above all rule and authority, power and dominion.
He is above every title that can be given,
Not only in the present age, but also in the age to come.
God has placed everything under his feet
And appointed him as ruler over all things.
He did all this for us, his church, his body.
We are the fullness of him who fills everything in every way.
In Jesus' name, amen.

Humbling Ourselves Before God

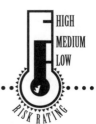

TOPIC: HUMILITY
SCRIPTURE: PHILIPPIANS 2:5-11

This activity can be used to remind participants to willingly respond to God's call in their lives.

A week or so before your sermon, ask creative members of the youth group (or another group in your church) to create a worship pantomime to be performed to the words of Philippians 2:5-11. Give each person a photocopy of the "Humble Before God" hand-out (p. 86). Tell the performers that they can perform the pantomime as it is written on the handout or they can alter it as they wish. Be sure to let the performers know that they won't be speaking. They'll simply do the motions as you read the passage aloud.

At the appropriate time in the sermon, have the performers join you in front of the congregation. Say: **I will be reading a passage from the book of Philippians that describes how Jesus responded to God's call on his life and how we, too, should respond to God. The performers will be visually representing the passage as I read it aloud.**

Read Philippians 2:5-11 slowly, pausing as needed to allow the performers to do their parts. Afterward, thank the performers and continue your sermon. As you speak, refer to the pantomime frequently to help illustrate the meaning of the passage.

The one suggestion for improvement that I'd share with people who deliver sermons is... Stick to the subject in a clear, memorable, creative way.

HUMBLE BEFORE GOD

- Your attitude should be the same as that of Christ Jesus *(stand with hands clasped and head down):*

- Who, being in very nature God *(lift head and look outward, sweeping hands out across the horizon, as though performing an act of creation)*

- did not consider equality with God something to be grasped, but made himself nothing *(quickly kneel, bow head, and cover head with crossed arms),*

- taking the very nature of a servant, being made in human likeness *(extend hands, cupping them together as though offering service).*

- And being found in appearance as a man *(look at arms in astonishment as though for the first time),*

- he humbled himself and became obedient to death—even death on a cross! *(While still kneeling, extend arms out as though nailed to a cross, and bow head.)*

- Therefore God highly exalted him to the highest place *(with arms still extended, stand and look up)*

- and gave him the name that is above every name *(raise arms toward heaven),*

- that at the name of Jesus every knee should bow, in heaven *(quickly bring arms down, then raise them toward heaven again)*

- and on earth *(extend arms toward the audience)*

- and under the earth *(spread arms downward toward the floor),*

- and every tongue confess that Jesus Christ is Lord *(kneel),*

- to the glory of God the Father. *(Raise arms and lift face toward heaven, smiling.)*

The Gift of God's Grace

HIGH
MEDIUM
LOW

RISK RATING

TOPIC: GRACE

SCRIPTURE: TITUS 3:4-7

Use this idea to help people experience God's grace in a creative way.

During the week before the service, ask six or eight people to come to church the following Sunday with white sheets that they can wear over their clothes. Assign partners, and ask each pair to bring two large bowls of warm water and a dry towel. In one of the bowls, ask volunteers to add a liquid skin cleanser. Tell each pair to be ready on your cue to enter the worship area and silently wash, rinse, and dry the hands of three or four individuals in the congregation. Encourage the pairs to choose individuals at random and to spread their choices around the whole worship area.

When Sunday comes, have the congregation stand. Read a prepared list of common sins such as lying, speeding, gossiping, and complaining. As you list the sins, instruct congregational members to silently meditate on their own sins.

After a few minutes, read aloud Titus 3:4-7. As you read, have the pairs enter and begin to quietly wash people's hands. Continue reading the passage again and again for three or four minutes.

When each pair of volunteers has finished washing the hands of three or four people, have members of the congregation each choose a partner and discuss these questions:

● **How did you react when people came in and started washing people's hands?**

● **How is that feeling similar to the way we sometimes feel before God?**

● **What can we learn from this passage about God's grace?**

After the discussion, continue your sermon.

HIGH
MEDIUM
LOW

RISK RATING

Weighty Journey

TOPIC: ENCUMBRANCES

SCRIPTURE: HEBREWS 12:1-3

Use this illustration to demonstrate that the things in life we think are essential may actually hold us back from serving God.

A week before the service, ask about ten volunteers to bring shoulder bags and backpacks to the church service. Ask them to stuff the bags or backpacks with lightweight items so the bags appear to be full. In addition, ask each volunteer to use paper, markers, and tape to label the baggage with one of the following "essentials" of life: money, career, marriage, car, house, entertainment, good reputation, friends, possessions, and plans for the future. Instruct the volunteers to sit in various places all around the worship area and to be ready to bring their bags to the stage when you ask for advice from the audience.

During the service, ask a young female volunteer to come to the stage. (You will want to set this up in advance so as not to embarrass anyone.)

Say: **We're going to help prepare you for life's journey. To do that, we'll need to provide things that the world says are essential to success. Does anyone in the congregation have an idea of what some of those keys to success are?**

At this point, have the volunteers each stand in turn and say, "I know something she needs." Then have each come to the front and hang his or her bag or backpack on her. After all ten volunteers have loaded her down, tell the volunteer: **Now you're ready for life's race. I want you to show us that you now know what you're doing. So I'd like you to run one time around the edge of the worship area. We'll all cheer you on as you go. Ready? Go fast!**

Encourage the volunteer to run as fast as she can around the worship area while carrying the bags. (She probably won't make it with all the bags. Just encourage her not to stop until she makes it back.)

After the race, ask the volunteer:

● **How'd you do? Explain.**

● **Did these essentials to success help you? Why or why not?**

VIEW FROM THE PEW

- **What does this tell us about successfully running life's race?**

Have the congregation offer a round of applause; then read aloud Hebrews 12:1-3. Refer to the illustration frequently to show that certain ideas and pursuits can prevent us from focusing on Christ and running a good race of faith.

"They say it's a tough church to preach at."

HIGH
MEDIUM
LOW

RISK RATING

Like Parent, Like Child

TOPIC: BEING LIKE CHRIST

SCRIPTURE: ROMANS 8:28-29

VIEW FROM THE PEW

The one suggestion for improvement that I'd share with people who deliver sermons is... Do something memorable! It's easy to forget what last week's sermon was about.

Use this activity to help people understand how we are transformed into the likeness of Christ.

At some point near the end of your sermon, have the participants form groups of four. Have group members take turns describing what their parents were like when the participants were kids. Then have them each share two or three unexpected ways they have turned out to be like their parents. Once everyone has shared, have groups discuss the following questions:

● How did you end up becoming like your parents in ways you didn't expect?

● How might that be similar to the way we, as Christians, become like Jesus over time?

● In what ways have you changed to be more like Jesus in the past year?

● What do you attribute these changes to?

● What do you think we will be like when Christ returns?

After the discussion, thank groups for participating, and continue your sermon.

A Blanket of Deceit

HIGH
MEDIUM
LOW

RISK RATING

TOPIC: GUILT

SCRIPTURE: PSALM 32

This activity demonstrates that sin and guilt have a remarkable way of causing people to walk in confusion.

Arrange for a volunteer to come to the platform with you at a specified time during your sermon. Tell the church that this person represents someone who has done something really bad, someone whose sin has kept him or her from seeing God clearly.

Say: **If you continue in sin, you will never reach the potential God has given you.**

Explain to the congregation that you are going to cover this person's head and shoulders with a blanket and encourage him or her to find God. Bring out a sign that has the word "God" written or painted on it.

Say: **After I've covered this person with a blanket, I'll place the sign somewhere in the room. The volunteer will listen to you as you shout instructions about where to find the sign. The task will be difficult because you can choose to either tell the truth or to lie about the sign's location.**

Place the sign somewhere in the worship area, and have people in the congregation begin shouting their instructions. The volunteer will undoubtedly struggle to no avail through this confusing process. After a short time, lift the blanket, and release the person to find the sign. Applaud the volunteer, and thank him or her for participating. Ask: **What point did this activity make?**

Say: **When we are covered by a blanket of guilt and sin, we are tempted to listen to everyone. As a result, we become self-focused and confused. Confessing our sins to God, however, removes the blanket of sin and releases us from darkness and confusion. We can then see God clearly once again and pursue him with passion.**

You may want to ask the congregation to respond to the following questions:

- What does guilt do to your ability to listen to God?
- What are the voices that you are tempted to listen to when guilt is in your life?
- How can we better "tune in" to God?

"I still think he could do more for the church."

Subtleties of Sin

HIGH
MEDIUM
LOW

RISK RATING

TOPIC: DISTRACTIONS

SCRIPTURE: EPHESIANS 6:11-12

The object of this activity is to demonstrate that sin creeps into people's lives a little at a time and distracts them from the truth. It develops as a skit in which two tempters try to distract you from preaching. You'll need several props including a large tarp, a movable podium (if you use a podium as you preach), a ladder, a sign with "Coming Soon: Sin!" written on it, a string of Christmas lights, two unlabeled cans of soup, a can opener, a pair of rubber boots, and a transparent dropcloth. Before the sermon, arrange for two volunteers to play the roles of the tempters.

After you read the Scripture passage to the congregation, the two tempters walk to the front of the worship area and spread a tarp on the floor. They wave to you and then leave. (After each appearance of the tempters, move a few steps closer to the tarp. If you use a podium of some kind, move it with you.)

After you continue to preach undistracted for a minute or so longer, the two tempters walk out, set a ladder on the tarp, and leave again. After another interval of preaching, the tempters again appear and place on the ladder the "Coming Soon: Sin!" sign. They wave and then leave.

The tempters enter again and this time decorate the ladder with Christmas lights. After another brief interval, they reappear with two unlabeled cans of soup. They open the cans, place them on top of the ladder, and then leave.

Finally, one tempter appears and places a pair of rubber boots on the tarp near where you are now standing. This time, however, he or she does not leave. After you've moved a little closer to the tarp, the tempter helps you remove your shoes and puts the boots on your feet.

Begin reading Ephesians 6:11-12. As you read, the tempters place a clean, transparent dropcloth over you. Keep talking about how easy it is to lose your focus and how things often become blurry.

Begin walking toward the ladder. When you reach it, the

VIEW FROM THE PEW

The one suggestion for improvement that I'd share with people who deliver sermons is... Involve the congregation's interest.

tempters dump the contents of the cans on you. (Be sure to hold onto the dropcloth so the contents will slide off.) After the tempters have finished dumping the soup, they give each other a high five and leave.

Continue your sermon about the need for Christians to wear the full armor of God and take a stand against the devil's schemes.

(**Note:** It is important for you to ignore the tempters until the very end. Casually begin to take more notice of them each time they appear. Be prepared, however, for your audience to pay more attention to them than to you. That's part of the point.)

"Of course, on the other hand, ..."

Sliced Bread

HIGH
MEDIUM
LOW

RISK RATING

TOPIC: PROVISION

SCRIPTURE: MARK 6:30-44

Use this idea to demonstrate God's abundant provision for his followers. To equate Jesus' use of five loaves to feed five thousand people to the number of loaves that would be needed for your congregation, complete the following equation. Multiply the number of people in a typical service by 5, (the number of loaves available to Jesus); then divide it by 5,000 (the number of people Jesus fed). For example, if you normally have 200 people in a service, multiply 200 by 5, which equals 1,000. Divide 1,000 by 5,000, which equals 0.2. (This process can be simplified by dividing the number of participants by 1,000.) Use the final number to estimate the amount of bread you will use for this illustration. For example, if your final number is 0.2, bring 20 percent of a loaf of bread or about four slices.

At the appropriate time during your sermon, say: **Consider this passage from the perspective of the disciples. Jesus has told you to feed the entire crowd of at least five thousand people. So you set off to do the work and come up with only five loaves of bread and two fish.**

It would be the same thing as Jesus telling me to feed everyone here with [amount of bread you have] **of bread. (Note:** You might want to take a moment to explain how you arrived at the amount of bread you have.)

Distribute the bread to the members of the congregation. Have them each tear off a small piece and pass the bread to someone else. Continue your sermon on Mark 6:30-44.

At the end of the sermon say:

● **Raise your hand if you didn't get any bread.**

● **Raise your hand if you had enough to consider it a full meal.**

Say: **That's the best we can do without Christ. But Jesus can turn our paltry efforts into a bountiful feast. The disciples gathered twelve basketfuls of bread and fish after five thousand people were well fed. Jesus' blessings and his provision are far beyond what we can do or even imagine.**

HIGH
MEDIUM
LOW

RISK RATING

Making Disciples

TOPIC: EVANGELISM

SCRIPTURE: MATTHEW 28:16-20

Use this idea to challenge your congregation to start reaching out to non-Christians who are in need of God's love. Make one photocopy of the handout on page 97 for everyone in the congregation. If possible, copy it onto card stock or thick paper, making the copies small enough to fit into a Bible.

At the appropriate time during your sermon, say: **I am going to give you an opportunity to start making a disciple right now.** Have ushers distribute the handouts to the congregation.

Say: **The cards that are being distributed have spaces for four names. Write down the names of non-Christians you believe you should reach out to. Before you write anything, take a few minutes to wait for God's direction. Just remain silent and listen with your heart while I pray for you. Please join me now in prayer.**

Lord, I ask you to bring the name of at least one non-Christian to every single person here. Please bring these people to mind as we wait for your direction. In Jesus' name...

Wait for about two minutes, then say: **Amen.** After the members of your congregation have written the names that God has brought to their minds, say: **You have a chance right now to begin making disciples of the people on your list. I'd like you to begin by praying for them. Ask God to show you how to begin reaching out to them. Take a minute or two to think about and write down a few ways that you can obey God's will for this area of your life.**

Allow your congregation to pray for a few minutes. Encourage the participants to keep their lists in their Bibles so that they remember to pray for and reach out to the people on their lists.

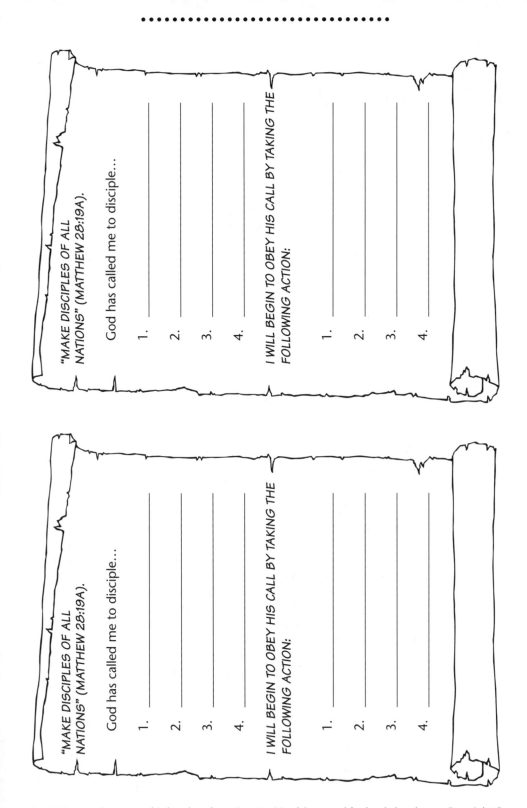

"MAKE DISCIPLES OF ALL NATIONS" (MATTHEW 28:19A).

God has called me to disciple…

1. _____

2. _____

3. _____

4. _____

I WILL BEGIN TO OBEY HIS CALL BY TAKING THE FOLLOWING ACTION:

1. _____

2. _____

3. _____

4. _____

"MAKE DISCIPLES OF ALL NATIONS" (MATTHEW 28:19A).

God has called me to disciple…

1. _____

2. _____

3. _____

4. _____

I WILL BEGIN TO OBEY HIS CALL BY TAKING THE FOLLOWING ACTION:

1. _____

2. _____

3. _____

4. _____

Suck It Up

TOPIC: SURVIVAL

SCRIPTURE: ISAIAH 40:21-31

Use this idea to demonstrate that God's ability to sustain us is far greater than our own ability to do so. You'll need one drinking straw and one uninflated balloon for each person in your congregation. You'll also need a box fan and a long extension cord. Before you use this idea, turn off ceiling fans, air conditioners, and forced-air heat in the worship area.

Have ushers distribute a drinking straw and a balloon to each person in your congregation. At the appropriate time during your sermon, ask your participants to blow up and tie off their balloons. Say: **Your balloon symbolizes the many different aspects of your life. In this illustration, you need to keep your life from crashing down, but you are allowed to use only your straw to do so. When I say "go," hold the balloon—your life—in front of you, put the straw in your mouth, and keep your life up as long as you can by sucking through the straw. Once you start sucking, you may not use your hands. Ready? Go!**

After several minutes, say: **That pretty much demonstrates your ability to sustain yourself.** Lift up the box fan so that everyone can see it. Turn it on (be careful not to put your fingers in the fan), and hold it up so that it blows upward. Ask a few participants to put their balloons above the fan so that the fan holds the balloons in place. Say: **This fan represents God; whereas the straw represents you. God can not only sustain you, he can do much more.** Ask the members of your congregation to throw their balloons into the air in the middle aisle. Run down the middle aisle with the fan, lifting as many balloons as high as possible.

Say: **By our own power, we can't even keep our lives together. God is able to do more than keep us going. He can catapult us to new heights. He can make us soar like eagles. Give God the balloon that represents your life so he can do something with it. Quit trying to keep it going on your own. You can't.**

Move into the next point of your sermon, and refer to the balloons as appropriate.

Round 'Em Up

HIGH
MEDIUM
LOW

RISK RATING

TOPIC: GOD'S CARE

SCRIPTURE: JOHN 10:11-18

Use this idea to help your congregation understand Christ's concern for his people and our need for him. Prepare one index card for each member of your congregation. For every ten people in your congregation, make one index card that says "shepherd," one that says "wolf," and eight that say "sheep." Have your ushers give one card to each person as he or she enters the worship area.

Read John 10:11-18 aloud, then say: **In order to better understand this parable, we're going to do a simulation. Look at the index card you received when you came in today. If your card says "sheep," your job is to wander around aimlessly, saying "baa." If your card says "shepherd," your job is to gather all the sheep together. You can direct your sheep by holding their hands and helping them along or by calling to them. Sheep should obey the shepherd, but remember: Sheep aren't too bright. Once the shepherd has put two or more sheep together, they stay together unless a wolf comes along and scatters them. If your card says "wolf," you must howl as you walk around. You are trying to scatter the sheep. To do that, come between any two sheep and howl. When you do that, those two sheep must scatter. Shepherds, all you have to do to control the wolves is to touch them. Once a shepherd touches a wolf, the wolf must whimper and stay in one place for fifteen seconds. Are there any questions? Ready? Begin.**

After about three minutes, have the members of your congregation debrief the experience by discussing these questions:

● **How did this activity demonstrate the truths of John 10:11-18?**

● **What was it like to be a wolf? a sheep? a shepherd?**

● **How was this activity like real life? different?**

Continue your sermon.

TOPICAL INDEX

RISK-RATING INDEX

Low-Risk Illustrations

Medium-Risk Illustrations

High-Risk Illustrations

RISK-RATING INDEX (CONTINUED)

High-Risk Illustrations

SCRIPTURE INDEX

Group Publishing, Inc.
Attention: Product Development
P.O. Box 481, Loveland, CO 80539
Fax: (970) 679-4370

Evaluation for *BORE NO MORE! 2*

Please help Group Publishing, Inc., continue to provide innovative and useful resources for ministry. Please take a moment to fill out this evaluation and mail or fax it to us. Thanks!

● ● ●

1. As a whole, this book has been (circle one)

not very helpful   very helpful

1   2   3   4   5   6   7   8   9   10

2. The best things about this book:

3. Ways this book could be improved:

4. Things I will change because of this book:

5. Other books I'd like to see Group publish in the future:

6. Would you be interested in field-testing future Group products and giving us your feedback? If so, please fill in the information below:

Name _____

Street Address _____

City_____State_____Zip _____

Phone Number _____Date _____

Exciting Resources for Your Adult Ministry

Sermon-Booster Dramas

Tim Kurth

Now you can deliver powerful messages in fresh, new ways. Set up your message with memorable, easy-to-produce dramas—each just 3 minutes or less! These 25 low-prep dramas hit hot topics ranging from burnout…ethics…parenting…stress…to work…career issues and more! Your listeners will be on the edge of their seats!

ISBN 0-7644-2016-X

Fun Friend-Making Activities for Adult Groups

Karen Dockrey

More than 50 relational programming ideas help even shy adults talk with others at church! You'll find low-risk Icebreakers to get adults introduced and talking…Camaraderie-Builders that help adults connect and start talking about what's really happening in their lives…and Friend-Makers to cement friendships with authentic sharing and accountability.

ISBN 0-7644-2011-9

Bore No More (For Every Pastor, Speaker, Teacher)

Mike & Amy Nappa

This is a must-have for pastors, college/career speakers, and others who address groups! Because rather than just provide illustrations to entertain audiences, the authors show readers how to involve audiences in the learning process. The 70 sermon ideas presented are based on New Testament passages, but the principles apply to all passages.

ISBN 1-55945-266-8

Young Adult Faith-Launchers

These 18 in-depth Bible studies are perfect for young adults who want to strengthen their faith and deepen their relationships. They will explore real-world issues…ask the tough questions…and along the way turn casual relationships into supportive, caring friendships. Quick prep and high involvement make these the ideal studies for peer-led Bible studies, small groups, and classes.

ISBN 0-7644-2037-2

Bible Study Series

Give Your Teenagers a Solid Faith Foundation That Lasts a Lifetime!

Here are the *essentials* of the Christian life—core values teenagers *must* believe to make good decisions now...and build an *unshakable* lifelong faith. Developed by youth workers like you...field-tested with *real* youth groups in *real* churches...here's the meat your kids *must* have to grow spiritually—presented in a fun, involving way!

Each 4-session **Core Belief Bible Study Series** book lets you easily...
- Lead deep, compelling, *relevant* discussions your kids won't want to miss...
- Involve teenagers in exploring life-changing truths...
- Help kids create healthy relationships with each other—and you!

Plus you'll make an *eternal difference* in the lives of your kids as you give them a solid faith foundation that stands firm on God's Word.

Here are the Core Belief Bible Study Series titles already available...

Senior High Studies

Why **Authority** Matters	0-7644-0892-5
Why **Being a Christian** Matters	0-7644-0883-6
Why **Creation** Matters	0-7644-0880-1
Why **Forgiveness** Matters	0-7644-0887-9
Why **God** Matters	0-7644-0874-7
Why **God's Justice** Matters	0-7644-0886-0
Why **Jesus Christ** Matters	0-7644-0875-5
Why **Love** Matters	0-7644-0889-5
Why **Our Families** Matter	0-7644-0894-1
Why **Personal Character** Matters	0-7644-0885-2
Why **Prayer** Matters	0-7644-0893-3
Why **Relationships** Matter	0-7644-0896-8
Why **Serving Others** Matters	0-7644-0895-X
Why **Spiritual Growth** Matters	0-7644-0884-4
Why **Suffering** Matters	0-7644-0879-8
Why **the Bible** Matters	0-7644-0882-8
Why **the Church** Matters	0-7644-0890-9
Why **the Holy Spirit** Matters	0-7644-0876-3
Why **the Last Days** Matter	0-7644-0888-7
Why **the Spiritual Realm** Matters	0-7644-0881-X
Why **Worship** Matters	0-7644-0891-7

Junior High/Middle School Studies

The Truth About **Authority**	0-7644-0868-2
The Truth About **Being a Christian**	0-7644-0859-3
The Truth About **Creation**	0-7644-0856-9
The Truth About **Developing Character**	0-7644-0861-5
The Truth About **God**	0-7644-0850-X
The Truth About **God's Justice**	0-7644-0862-3
The Truth About **Jesus Christ**	0-7644-0851-8
The Truth About **Love**	0-7644-0865-8
The Truth About **Our Families**	0-7644-0870-4
The Truth About **Prayer**	0-7644-0869-0
The Truth About **Relationships**	0-7644-0872-0
The Truth About **Serving Others**	0-7644-0871-2
The Truth About **Sin and Forgiveness**	0-7644-0863-1
The Truth About **Spiritual Growth**	0-7644-0860-7
The Truth About **Suffering**	0-7644-0855-0
The Truth About **the Bible**	0-7644-0858-5
The Truth About **the Church**	0-7644-0899-2
The Truth About **the Holy Spirit**	0-7644-0852-6
The Truth About **the Last Days**	0-7644-0864-X
The Truth About **the Spiritual Realm**	0-7644-0857-7
The Truth About **Worship**	0-7644-0867-4

Order today from your local Christian bookstore, or write:
Group Publishing, P.O. Box 485, Loveland, CO 80539.

TEACH YOUR PRESCHOOLERS AS JESUS TAUGHT WITH GROUP'S *HANDS-ON BIBLE CURRICULUM*™

Hands-On Bible Curriculum™ **for preschoolers** helps your preschoolers learn the way they learn best—by touching, exploring, and discovering. With active learning, preschoolers love learning about the Bible, and they really remember what they learn.

Because small children learn best through repetition, Preschoolers and Pre-K & K will learn one important point per lesson, and Toddlers & 2s will learn one point each month with **Hands-On Bible Curriculum**. These important lessons will stick with them and comfort them during their daily lives. Your children will learn:

- •God is our friend,
- •who Jesus is, and
- •we can always trust Jesus.

The **Learning Lab**® is packed with age-appropriate learning tools for fun, faith-building lessons. Toddlers & 2s explore big **Interactive StoryBoards**™ with enticing textures that toddlers love to touch—like sandpaper for earth, cotton for clouds, and blue cellophane for water. While they hear the Bible story, children also *touch* the Bible story. And they learn. **Bible Big Books**™ captivate Preschoolers and Pre-K & K while teaching them important Bible lessons. With **Jumbo Bible Puzzles**™ and involving **Learning Mats**™, your children will see, touch, and explore their Bible stories. Each quarter there's a brand-new collection of supplies to keep your lessons fresh and involving.

Fuzzy, age-appropriate hand puppets are also available to add to the learning experience. What better way to teach your class than with the help of an attention-getting teaching assistant? These child-friendly puppets help you teach each lesson with scripts provided in the **Teacher Guide**. Plus, your children will enjoy teaching the puppets what they learn. Cuddles the Lamb, Whiskers the Mouse, and Pockets the Kangaroo turn each lesson into an interactive and entertaining learning experience.

Just order one **Learning Lab** and one **Teacher Guide** for each age level, add a few common classroom supplies, and presto—you have everything you need to inspire and build faith in your children. For more interactive fun, introduce your children to the age-appropriate puppet who will be your teaching assistant and their friend. No student books are required!

Hands-On Bible Curriculum is also available for elementary grades.

Order today from your local Christian bookstore, or write: Group Publishing, P.O. Box 485, Loveland, CO 80539.